"What About Us?"

The end-time calling of Gentiles in Israel's revival

EITAN SHISHKOFF

Illustrations at the beginning of each chapter
by Connie Kind Shishkoff (ckspaint@gmail.com)

Cover Design by David Coddington (codgraf@mevohama.org.il)

Burkhart Books
Bedford, Texas
www.burkhartbooks.com

Dedication

I would like to dedicate this book to my mother and father, Muriel Mendelsohn Shishkoff and Nicholas Simeon Shishkoff (both, 1917-2011). They nurtured me, taught me, and gave me their heart for the human race. I only regret not being able to hand them a first-run copy in person. But, I know they would have been proud, and it gives me great joy to honor them in this way.

Contents

Foreword

Eitan has lived/is living what he is writing. He is a part of the growing worldwide cycle of revival between the Church and Israel, believers in Jesus from the nations and the resurrected community of Jewish believers in their Messiah Yeshua. As a Jewish believer who lives in Israel, he has an exceptional vantage point for weaving together experience with Scripture, showing the necessity of this union of Jew and non-Jew in preparation for Jesus' return.

When Paul was writing to the early Roman believers, he cautioned them again and again concerning their relationship to their Jewish brothers and sisters through whom they had received redemption. "Has God rejected His people?" he asked, then responded to his own question, "Not at all!...God has not rejected His people whom He foreknew...Did they stumble so as to fall beyond recovery? Not at all! Rather because of their transgression, salvation has come to the Gentiles (those from the nations) to make Israel envious. But if their transgression means riches for the world and their loss means riches for the Gentiles, how much greater riches will their fullness bring!" (Romans 11:1, 11-12)

Paul saw that the "fullness" of Israel would bring greater riches to the nations. A few verses later Paul says, "Israel has experienced a hardness in part until the fullness of the Gentiles has come in, and so all Israel will be saved." Something about the fullness of the nations brings about the salvation of Israel. But the fullness of Israel also brings greater riches to the nations. The fullness of Israel and the fullness of the nations—that is the subject of Eitan's book.

It was Eitan who first compelled me to take a harder look at the ancient biblical story of Ruth and Boaz, and to see in them this same key to world redemption as we draw nearer to the reappearance of Jesus, as King of all the earth.

When Ruth, the non-Jew, entered into a covenant with Boaz, the Jew, they brought forth the Kingdom of David through whom this Jewish Messiah and World Redeemer came.

Today Boaz has risen from the dead in the form of Jewish believers, who are back on the scene after centuries of absence. At the same time, today's Ruth, believers in Jesus from all the nations, is awakening to the presence of Boaz, and is growing in love for him.

When today's Ruth acknowledges her Boaz and enters into covenant with him, we will see the return of David's Greater Son, Yeshua (Jesus).

Let Eitan show you some of the ways it is happening and how you can become actively involved in this divinely ordained marriage.

Don Finto
President, Caleb Company
Pastor Emeritus, Belmont Church
Author of *Your People Shall be My People*

Introduction

"Hey, What About Us? What About the Gentiles?"

The sincere, middle-aged North American woman who asked me this question had been journeying with us all over Israel along with 137 other curious Christians and Messianic Jews. They were visiting Israeli Messianic congregations and Biblical/Zionist sites. She was witnessing firsthand the phenomenal rebirth of faith in *Yeshua*[1] (Jesus) among Israeli Jews, both native-born and immigrant. Her heart was touched and she wanted to participate in Israel's redemption, to be more than a passive spectator.

The purpose of this book is to answer her question. It is a good question, an important question. If God has left the non-Jewish followers of Jesus out of Israel's historic/prophetic awakening, something's wrong. If in Israel's rediscovery of the most famous Jew of all time, our Messiah King, there's no place for His Gentile disciples to be involved, it leaves most of God's family out of the celebration.

Yet, thankfully, this is not the case. In fact, the Scriptures speak vividly and with inspiration of an end-time partnership between Jewish and Gentile believers in Yeshua. The precedents for such a partnership abound in the Hebrew Scriptures and in the New Covenant. I have been privileged to experience the deep joys of this partnership first hand, around the world. I want to share those stories with you and to explore foundational passages from the Scriptures that provide a strong theological understanding of our mutual dependence.

It is that interdependence which provides the key to answering the question "What about the Gentiles?" Simply stated, we need each other. We Messianic Jews cannot fulfill our God-given role in hastening Yeshua's return without our Gentile brethren. Nor can they realize the age-old dream of God's kingdom established on earth without us. My prayerful hope is that through this book a friendship will be fostered. That has been the divine plan all along. We were tragically separated in the early centuries of this era. Yeshua's original community began with Jewish disciples in first-century Israel. Then, the door was opened to the Gentiles by the Apostles, as recorded in the Book of Acts. That short-lived, unity without uniformity was ended by religious leaders on both sides. The rabbis said "You can't believe in Jesus and be Jewish." The bishops said "You can't be a Christian and do Jewish stuff." But they were both wrong. This was an unscriptural, unintended uprooting of faith in Yeshua:

- From its original and eternal roots in the Hebrew Bible,
- From Israel's history, and
- From the prophetic expectation of the exiles' return and revival.

Historians validate with one voice that Yeshua's first followers and the early congregations were fully Jewish, celebrating the Torah of Israel, looking for the fulfillment of her prophets' words.

Now, some twenty centuries later, we have returned to the land. As Israeli citizens, we are walking with Yeshua as our Messiah. And the signs of His return are appearing daily. But what about the Gentiles? Is their time over?

...And Jerusalem will be trampled by Gentiles until the times of the Gentiles are fulfilled. Luke 21:24

...blindness in part has happened to Israel until the fullness of the Gentiles has come in. Romans 11:25

Is that what Luke and Paul meant? Or is there a shared "Jewish-Gentile" mission at the end? There is a mystery here that is to be revealed in these times (see Ephesians 3:4-6 and 2:19-22). Yeshua's disciples from both Jewish and non-Jewish families are being handed an unprecedented opportunity to overturn the dreadfully wrong division between us, and then to welcome back the King as His covenant friends, deeply committed to each other. I believe that we have a rare chance to show Israel and the nations of the world the nature of humility and mutual serving. I believe that both of us have been given a high and thrilling calling.

As a Messianic Jew who has been involved in Jewish ministry for over 30 years, I've had the adventure of participating in the historic awakening of Jewish people to faith in Jesus. This phenomenon has been attracting increasing interest among the Lord's Gentile disciples around the world. What began in the 1970s as distant curiosity has become a growing passion globally, to explore the Jewish roots of New Covenant faith and to further God's purposes for Israel.

Since immigrating to Israel in 1992, a significant portion of my work has focused on responding to the desire of Gentile Christians to assist in Israel's salvation. On every continent Christians are praying earnestly for Israel—crying out to God that we will find Yeshua as our Messiah King. While traveling to numerous countries, I've experienced this amazing love for the Jewish people within the Gentile Church. During more than two decades I have personally interacted with tens of thousands of Christians from hundreds of groups in a wide variety of denominations on five continents. The level of interest, care and honor given to us as Israeli believers is humbling and, at times, almost embarrassing.

In fact, there are churches where worshipers wave tambourines with stars of David, where Israeli flags are proudly displayed and the call of the ram's horn (*shofar*) is heard. Until very recently in the history of Christianity this combination of Gentile Christians and Jewish symbolism was virtually unknown. Why is this happening now? And what are the implications for the life of the Church? As a Messianic Jew and as an Israeli, I cannot but view positively this newfound attraction for things Jewish. Yeshua has been painfully cut off from His Jewish roots for some 1800 years. So, this recent development is a refreshing change in Church history, to say the least. In a welcome turn of events, the Church is rediscovering her own origin in the ancient soil of God's promises to Abraham, Isaac and Jacob.

Causes for Concern

Yet for all the celebration, there are also causes for concern. Many are confused. Are Gentile believers to adopt the Mosaic Law as their requisite pattern of life? Should the Church yield to mainstream Jewish demands that evangelism be off limits because of the ugly anti-Semitic past? Is there a separate salvation covenant for Israel that removes the necessity of faith in Yeshua? How is the Church to relate to Israel...or to the remarkable movement of Jews embracing Jesus? These and many other questions call for thoughtful answers. At stake is not only the health of the body of Christ, but the salvation of Israel.

I want to address this extraordinary hour of destiny. It's a "setup" from God. I believe He opened the eyes of my generation of Jewish seekers, refugees of the wild and woolly cultural revolution of the 1960s. When we saw Jesus (this happened to me literally) we knew He was the true answer to all we sought. Then, many of us returned to our Jewish heritage, as members of the universal body of Christ.

Realizing that a special work of grace was taking place, some of our Gentile brethren encouraged us to live an authentic Jewish life in Yeshua. I simply could not have fulfilled my calling without them. In the decades since, God has used precious brothers and sisters from the nations to give us in-depth ministry training, abundant financial resourcing, and steadfast intercessory backing. At the same time, I began seeing concrete evidence in Scripture that this was God's plan all along. I am convinced that the partnership of Yeshua's Gentile and Jewish followers is essential for the salvation of Israel, and thus for the Second Coming of Messiah.

We have a unique, history-making opportunity as Jewish and Gentile followers of Jesus the Messiah. His plan is to bring us into covenant friendship—to share His cup, to share in priestly intercession for the sake of Israel's redemption and to share in restoring the presence of God in Israel…just as King Solomon and King Hiram did when they teamed up to build the First Temple.

Eitan Shishkoff

Chapter One

The Hiram Factor

How a Gentile King Helped Bring the Glory of God to Israel

Now Hiram king of Tyre sent his servants to Solomon, because he heard that they had anointed him king in place of his father, for Hiram always loved David. 1 Kings 5:1

Our first meeting place as a new Israeli Messianic congregation was an aging warehouse, of 200 square meters (2,000 sq. ft.). One night in October of 1997, two years after we opened, the place was firebombed. In ways that we could not have predicted, this event became a dramatic turning point. Prayers and unsolicited gifts from many parts of the world began pouring in as people heard about the attack. Amazingly, within only sixty days of the arson, we signed a rent/purchase contract on a brand new building only fifty meters from the run-down warehouse that had been bombed.

To make the new empty space usable, we needed extensive interior construction. We had no money to hire Israeli architects and contractors. Miraculously, we had been given the funds to buy a portion of the space, but it was a stretch just to meet the increased rent and utilities. Just then several churches in the States, with whom we had close relationships, asked if we needed a team of carpenters and electricians! So, in the summer of 1998, men from far-away America showed up with their construction tools and big grins, saying "OK, let's get started." For us, it was a direct fulfillment of Isaiah 60:10 *"The sons of foreigners shall build up your walls..."* Again, in the year 2000, when we expanded into the other half of the building, teams came from Gentile nations to lay ceramic tiles, build walls and create a sanctuary that has been our "tent of meeting" ever since. Our use of the building, for both congregational and humanitarian aid purposes, has grown miraculously—to ten times the size of the original bombed warehouse.

This cooperative partnership has long been His plan. The God of Abraham, Isaac and Jacob loves to join Jew and Gentile in Messiah to bring God's kingdom to earth, and to the land of Israel in particular. One of the greatest building projects in all history was achieved by the partnership of a Jewish king and a Gentile king. It serves as a model for us now and forms the biblical backbone of this book.

One of my favorite characters in the Bible is King Hiram. He's the guy who built David's house (1 Kings 5:11). When Solomon inherited David's throne, he turned to Hiram for help in building a house for God (2 Samuel 7:12,13). This was the house "for His name" which the Lord had promised David would be built through his son.

Tyre - Hiram's City

Just up the coast of Israel, less than an hour's drive from where I live, lies Tyre, capital of King Hiram's ancient domain. Since there's not exactly a welcome mat waiting for those holding Israeli passports to come visit Lebanon, I've never been inside the country. But I hear that it's beautiful and that some of the legendary cedars of Lebanon still stand.

I am intrigued by this man, Hiram. It seems that destiny, the receptivity of King David, and his own heart, brought Hiram into a covenant friendship with the kings of Israel. Who was he? How did he become the "co-builder" of the Temple in Jerusalem?

We don't have much of a biography on Hiram. He's first mentioned in 2 Samuel 5:11 as sending cedars, masons and carpenters to build a house for King David. Then comes the deeper, relational statement: *"Hiram had always loved David"* (1 Kings 5:1).

Hiram was the king of Tyre, or today's southern district of Lebanon. Originally, the city of Tyre was populated on the mainland, with the island of Tyre just offshore and a much smaller island between the mainland and the larger island. The city was actually a minor community and, in fact, had to be founded and re-founded by neighboring Sidon. The island population, while small, had to rely on shipments of water and food from the mainland communities.

Hiram's reign (969 to 936 BCE) brought massive changes. He had cisterns and other engineering works built to catch and save rainwater (the first known in history). He joined the two islands together with landfill from the mainland (bringing it to an area of about 40 acres/160,000 sq. meters) and used some of the soil to enclose the harbor on the north side of the island, which enabled him to add mighty shipyards. He not only built the royal palace, but the world famous temples to Melkart and Astarte as well. Hundreds of years later, Herodotus wrote of them and Alexander the Great chose to worship there after he conquered Tyre in 332 BCE. The building of the main marketplace is, by tradition, credited to Hiram. This was near the northern harbor. He put a great deal of diplomatic effort into his relations with Israel, making his city Israel's main trading partner.

Hiram came to power in a modest little town and transformed it into the most important port on the Mediterranean. According to H. J. Katzenstein, "It was Hiram who laid the foundations for the great Tyrian Sea Empire that knew no equal in ancient history."[2] The 'Golden Age' of Phoenicia/Tyre began during his reign, but it wasn't all his doing. Tyre was aided by the waning power of Egypt, by the defeat of the

Philistines in 975 by David, and by the unification of Israel. Israel was a state friendly to Tyre (Hiram's diplomatic skills contributed). Since Israel possessed few ships, yet had access to land trade routes with Mesopotamia and a large market of customers for Tyre's trade, she became a steady ally.

Could the Temple have been built without King Hiram? We'll never know, but Solomon apparently felt that his Gentile neighbor's help was essential. King Solomon responded to Hiram's delegation (1 Kings 5:1) in the next verses by sending Hiram a letter:

> *And behold, I propose to build a house for the name of the Lord my God, as the Lord spoke to my father David, saying "Your son, whom I will set on your throne in your place, he shall build the house for my name." Now therefore, command that they cut down cedars for me from Lebanon; and I will pay you wages for your servants according to whatever you say. For you know there is none among us who has skill to cut timber like the Sidonians.* 1 Kings 5:5-6

Hiram rejoiced greatly at this proposal and, commending Solomon's wisdom, wrote back saying *"I will do all you desire concerning the cedar and cypress logs"* (1 Kings 5:8b). He promised to float the timber along the seacoast from Lebanon. Thus began a partnership that resulted in the Temple being constructed on Mount Moriah. When it was dedicated seven years later, the glory of God filled the house to such an extent that the priests couldn't perform their ministry because of the weight of God's intense presence.

This is such a vivid picture of what the Lord is after today. He wants to restore His glory to Israel. His pattern for doing so is laid out clearly in the account of Solomon and Hiram building the Temple together. Here are the steps in their unfolding partnership.

1. Friendship (1 Kings 5:1)

The whole project began with a deep friendship between David and Hiram. This is the first step, the foundation: friendship. David was the king whom Hiram "always loved," and who was the devoted father of Solomon. In the prophetic language of the Hebrew Scriptures, David's name is often used interchangeably with Messiah. Hiram, the Gentile king, and Solomon, the Jewish king, were joined by their mutual love for David, to whom was promised a Son who would rule forever, the Messiah. In this I see a perfect picture of us as Messianic Jews and Gentiles. We have been united through our common passion for Yeshua.

2. Timing (1 Kings 5:3)

King Solomon referenced his father's calling to build a house for God, yet his father's war-stained hands required the next generation for the actual building. I understand Solomon. I was born in 1948, the same year as re-born Israel. I sense something of the Lord's timing in having returned to Israel in this generation, after my family had been exiles from the land for untold generations. When I was still being challenged to check out Yeshua, I was told to look at His prophecy in Matthew 24:32-33.

Now learn this parable from the fig tree: when its branch has already become tender and puts forth leaves, you know that summer is near. So you also, when you see all these things, know that it is near—at the doors!

It rang true. I readily accepted that Israel was the fig tree and that my destiny was intertwined with this new/ancient nation due to the timing of my birth, which coincided with Israel's rebirth.

3. Vision (1 Kings 5:5)

...I propose to build a house for the name of the Lord my God, as the Lord spoke to my father, David, saying, "Your son, whom I will set on your throne in your place, he shall build the house for my name."

This was a big vision. Israel's king knew that he could not, should not, go it alone. So he inaugurated a joint "building project." Hiram was not jealous of Solomon's calling or position as David's natural son. Nor was Solomon too proud to ask Hiram for help. Their mutual trust and acceptance of each other's roles enabled them to serve God's higher goal of bringing His cloud of glory from heaven to Jerusalem. Think of it. A Jew and a Gentile were drawn together to establish a house for God. This house was to be a house of worship, a capital of priestly ministry unto the Living God. It was dedicated to the manifestation of God's presence on earth, with a center in Jerusalem. That speaks to me of what is going to happen at the end of the age. Once again, history will conform to God's intention, His vision, His visitation. The divine plan is to restore His glory to this earth. *"For the earth shall be full of the knowledge of the Lord as the waters cover the sea"* (Isaiah 11:9). He's recruiting us to be used as were Solomon and Hiram. The combination of Jew and Gentile brings God's presence when we walk in covenant friendship.

4. Strategy (1 Kings 5:6)

A large amount of resources had to be moved to provide for this construction project. Many people got involved in the process. In our generation, it's also going to take a lot of people, hearing God's voice and responding, to see Israel redeemed.

The fruit of God's strategy is joy. *"...when Hiram heard the words of Solomon...he rejoiced greatly"* (1 Kings 5:7). This is God's heart: bringing

His kids together to establish His presence on earth.

Both Hiram's and Solomon's portions in building the Temple were essential, but Hiram's is less understood. His role in constructing a house for God's glory was vital. So is that of every Gentile believer in bringing David's greater Son, to establish His Messianic kingdom. In the course of these pages you will find keys to participate in Israel's spiritual rebirth. No longer will her momentous restoration to the stage of world history be a distant event. Rather, you can find your valuable role in the miracle that is already under way.

What is the role of Gentiles in Israel's redemption? The story of two kings, Hiram and Solomon, is a prophetic picture that provides an answer to this crucial question. Their story holds the key to our partnership as Christians and Messianic Jews. What intrigues me is that Solomon, perhaps the most powerful king of his day, called upon Hiram, who ruled over a much smaller district to the north of Israel, asking him for help. What possible inspiration or pattern can we draw from their relationship? And how are we to proceed, in light of the immense challenges before us? I believe that God wants to enlighten us and to lead us in a very similar shared adventure.

Gentile Kings and Jewish Visionaries

Solomon and Hiram are not the only Jew and Gentile in Scripture who team up to bring restoration to Israel. Zerubbabel had his Cyrus, followed by Darius. Nehemiah was surely yoked with Artaxerxes for Israel's sake. This pair of Israel's visionary pioneers, not incidentally, was called to restore the Temple that Solomon and Hiram had built. The Book of Ezra opens with a radical statement by the Persian king, Cyrus.

All the kingdoms of the earth the Lord God has given me. And He has commanded me to build Him a house at Jerusalem which is in Judah. Who is among you of all His people? May his God be with him, and let him go up to Jerusalem which is in Judah, and build the house of the Lord God of Israel (He is God) which is in Jerusalem. And whoever is left in any place where he dwells, let the men of his place help him with silver and gold, with goods and livestock, besides the freewill offerings for the house of God, which is in Jerusalem. Ezra 1:2-4

This proclamation was taken throughout Cyrus's kingdom as fulfillment of Jeremiah's prophecy, that God would cause Israel to return after seventy years of exile in Babylon (Jeremiah 29:10; Ezra 1:1). The direct way this Gentile king states his instructions from God is radical. Clearly, this was no mere political move. It was a divinely mandated involvement. Something about Israel's physical and spiritual restoration calls for the strategic inclusion of tuned-in Gentiles.

Cyrus also took the 5,400 temple articles of silver and gold that had been stolen by Babylon 70 years earlier, and gave them to Sheshbazzar, the prince of Judah, to take back to Jerusalem (Ezra 1:7-11). My personal view is that these costly and precious items represent the gifts and the power of God intended for fruitful use in Israel, the original locus of God's supernatural activity on the earth. It is now time for these exquisite endowments to return to their original home, from centuries of "storage" among His children in the Church.

Cyrus's successor, Darius, confirmed his decree in the face of heavy opposition from the local governor (Ezra 5:3; 6:6). In the process he added:

Let the work of this house of God alone; let the governor of the Jews and the elders of the Jews build this house of God on its site...Let the cost be paid at the king's expense...that they may offer sacrifices of sweet aroma to the God of heaven... Ezra 6:7-8, 10

The language here echoes within me as a preview of our generation,

when the community of Messiah is being rebuilt on its original site, Israel, where Yeshua's disciples began! Again, God is
raising up visionary Gentiles who are extending their physical
resources, prayer, and covenant commitment to assist in the rebuilding.

Nehemiah pursued Jerusalem's restoration with passion. His
relationship with King Artaxerxes was so close that Nehemiah was
his cupbearer. Nehemiah's weeping burden for Jerusalem and the
ultimate fulfillment of God's kingdom compelled him to seek the
king's aid. The king was pleased to send him and provisioned the
passionate intercessor with timber, highway passage, and an army
escort. Thus Nehemiah rebuilt the wall around the city in fifty-two
days, overcoming persistent opposition and hardship. The partner-
ships of Zerubbabel/Cyrus-Darius and Nehemiah/Artaxerxes were
required to restore the Temple built by Solomon and Hiram, and its
host city, Jerusalem. These dramatic "matchups" changed history.

A Gentile king played an essential role in building the first Temple
in Jerusalem. King Hiram teamed up with King Solomon in a kingdom partnership that brought the glory of God from heaven to earth.
Their relationship is at the heart of this book. In the pages to come, I
am inviting you to discover your calling as a "Hiram" or a "Solomon."
Hiram's portion in constructing the Temple was indispensable. The role
of today's Gentile "builders" is just as important. Together, as Jew and
Gentile, we can hasten the arrival of David's greater Son to establish
the Messianic kingdom. In the course of this book you will find keys to
participate in Israel's spiritual rebirth. No longer will her momentous
restoration to the stage of world history be a distant event. Rather, you
can find your valuable role in the miracle that is already under way.

Chapter Two

God's Heart for All Mankind

His Plan Involves Every Nation Under Heaven

Moreover, concerning a foreigner, who is not of your people Israel, but has come from a far country for your name's sake (for they will hear of your great name and your strong hand and your outstretched arm), when he comes and prays toward this temple: then hear in heaven your dwelling place, and do according to all for which the foreigner calls to you, that all peoples of the earth may know your name and fear you, as do your people Israel...
1 Kings 8:41-43

The tribes and nations of the world captured my interest when I was still a boy. I thought it was fascinating that there were many different tribes and types of people. And I recognized two things. The first is that every group is special and unique. And the second is that all of mankind is one. As I began to study in school, I was intrigued by this subject. I kept seeking some way to bring everybody together. The logical place to look was the ever-available arena of political solutions.

As a high school student in the early 1960s I had a penchant for world peace. The concept of one benign government that could unify the globe in justice and compassion appealed to me. I even wrote a research paper "modestly" entitled "One World Government." After graduation, I advanced to the draft-dodging, demonstrating-in-the-streets phase. By the end of 1968 I had failed to unify the world. It was time to drop out of society and aid world peace by living on a country commune. At that point I thought that if everyone would simply move out of the cities and live on tribal farms, the world would be one—in peace and total harmony. Guided by naive vision and the love of newlyweds, I headed for New Mexico with my bride, Connie. We settled in a deserted valley outside of Albuquerque, in the foothills of Sandia Mountain.

Some of our first "neighbors" were the rattlesnakes that had wintered in the walls of the cellar we cleaned out and moved into. Our misadventures included life-threatening disease, temperatures of 40 below zero Fahrenheit (without the wind chill factor!) and a homemade roof that caved in and would have killed us and our infant son, had we been in the structure at the time.

It wasn't until I met Yeshua, the Prince of Peace, after four long years of rural commune pioneering, that my dreams found fulfillment. I read in the Bible:

> In your seed [Abraham's], _all the nations_ of the earth will blessed. Genesis 22:18

> Unto us a son is given and the [world's] government will be upon His shoulder. Isaiah 9:6

Here was God's plan for a truly blessed world, united under one government. My original concept had not been far off, but the most important feature was missing. I didn't know the Governor.

The universal need for true salvation—core transformation in each person—begs for a solution that leaves no one out. In fact, before Yeshua revealed Himself to me, that was one of my personal requirements for a "truth system." It had to include everybody. The uniqueness and variety of mankind's tribes have always inspired me. Whatever ultimate truth turned out to be, I was sure that it must be relevant for every tribe, language and category of human being.

So you can imagine how valuable it was for me to find Jesus. I had never read Ephesians 3:15, which gives praise to the Father of the Lord Yeshua, *"from whom the whole family in heaven and earth is named."* Otherwise, I would have known that all mankind receives life from God. I would have known that we are all created in His image, and that He is the source of our oneness. As the Father of the entire human family, God's heart is for all mankind. In order to understand the role of Gentiles in the salvation of Israel, we need to go back to the beginning and understand the breadth of God's heart. If we only focus on Israel, we forget that God loves all of the other nations. Then we are not relating to the true God.

The quote that headlines this chapter is taken from King Solomon's dedication of the Temple, which he built with the Gentile, King Hiram. In this momentous prayer, he asks the God of Israel to hear the prayers prayed by non-Jews. In the context of the 1Kings 8 dedication ceremony, he makes this request on behalf of those "foreigners" who are praying toward the First Temple in Jerusalem. We live nearly twenty centuries after the destruction of the Second Temple that replaced it. Therefore, I believe the latter portion of his prayer expresses the Lord's heart even more fully: *"…that all peoples of the earth may know your name and fear you…"* (1 Kings 8:43). Solomon realized God's concern for all the nations of the earth. He knew that the purpose of the Temple he had just built—and the very heart of God—was not only for the nation of Israel, but for all the world.

The Lord has given me a great privilege in life—that of sharing the gospel with many different kinds of people. As a messenger of Yeshua, I've spent time with Native American tribes, Hispanic people in the Southwest USA, convicts in a penitentiary, numerous nations in Europe, Asia, Africa and South America, hippie rebels like I was, and of course with Jewish people. What I have discovered is this: God has an intense love for every tribe and nation. The story of the Bible is the story of God's love for messed-up people of all kinds. According to 2 Peter 3:9, God is not willing for anyone to be lost, but for all to come to repentance. You cannot find a human being in all the earth that God does not care about. And this Father's love is critical for us to understand if we are to enter securely into His purposes as Jews and Gentiles.

"In Your Seed All Nations will be Blessed"

God's universal purposes were radically advanced through His first conversation with Abram. The Lord announced that through this man all the nations of the earth would be blessed (Genesis 12:1-3). He left his home in ancient Chaldea, directed only by his conversations with God. Abram's subsequent name change to Abraham (father of a multitude) proclaims his prophetic mandate to bring salvation to the whole world. God's heart was not just for Abram's family. Four thousand years ago God wanted to save the whole world. The patriarch's willingness to sacrifice his son provoked God.

Because you have done this thing, and have not withheld your son, your only son...In your seed all the nations of the earth shall be blessed. Genesis 22:16, 18

The New Testament opens with a stunning statement. *"The book of the genealogy of Yeshua the Messiah, the Son of David, the Son of Abraham"* (Matthew 1:1). Two thousand years after God began His friendship with Abraham, the seed of Abraham came to Israel. That seed is Jesus. God so loved all the families of the earth that He sent the seed of Abraham, His Son, to save the world (John 3:16).

Clearly, it is God's prerogative to choose one nation through which to bring redemption to the entire world. This is just what He did. Jesus, a descendant of Abraham, said *"salvation is of the Jews."* However, this "chosen" status can create misunderstanding and even resentment. On the one hand, deadly anti-Semitism arises from human jealousy and the Enemy's hatred of what God loves. On the other hand, some Christian believers, feeling envious of Jewish "chosenness," have felt a need to overly identify with and even convert to Judaism.

World Redemption = God's Ultimate Aim

All the way back in Moses' time, while focusing on Israel, God was aiming at world redemption. If we listen to the Lord's proclamation, which immediately preceded the Ten Commandments, we can hear His heart for all mankind.

You have seen what I did to the Egyptians, and how I bore you on eagles' wings and brought you to myself. Now therefore, if you will indeed obey my voice and keep my covenant, then you shall be a special treasure to me above all people; for all the earth is mine. And you shall be to me a kingdom of priests and a holy nation. Exodus 19:4-6

By saying *"all the earth is mine"* the Lord made it clear that this priesthood was not just for Israel, but for all nations.

That's why, in dedicating the Temple, King Solomon called upon the God of Israel to answer the prayers of all men everywhere who turn to Him. God's redemption plan included all nations from the very beginning. From the first chapters of Genesis, God declares the universality of His plan to redeem mankind, long before the categories of Jew and Gentile existed. This emphasizes the high value the Lord places on EVERY human being. It's inescapable. NO ONE will be left out of the action in the "final minutes of the game."

God our Savior...desires all men to be saved and to come to the knowledge of the truth. 1 Timothy 2:3-4

Only by gaining God's heart for all nations can we understand the world scene and be used together in the last days, as the 21st century equivalents of Hiram and Solomon. Hiram's role demonstrated the unique way in which that plan was to bring together Israel and the nations.

Light to the Gentiles

Called up to the mountain to meet with God, Moses was given a defining message for Israel. After laying claim to Israel as His special possession, the Lord mentions that He is the possessor of all the earth. He specifies that Israel is appointed to serve as priests, a holy nation in the midst of all the earth. We have a servant role among the nations. Yes, there is something special about the Jewish people. God says so without apology. But our election carries a weighty and sacred responsibility: bringing redemption to the rest of the world. I can't help but recall the words of Tevya the milkman in "Fiddler on the Roof," the play and movie based on Sholem Aleichem's immortal tales of Jewish communities in Eastern Europe. He is contemplating this not-always-easy calling, the responsibility to reflect the holiness of the Most High in the midst of a far less-than-perfect world. "Lord, I know that we are the chosen people. But just for once couldn't you choose someone else?"

As if answering Tevya's dilemma, one Jewish man did not shrink back from the weight of this calling. It was Yeshua. He bore the full pain and suffering, not only of the Jewish people, but of all mankind. The key that unlocks world slavery is the Messiah, Yeshua. His mission must include all nations, otherwise He is not the true Redeemer of Israel. Here are His own words, declared by Isaiah:

And now the Lord says, who formed me from the womb to be His Servant, to bring Jacob back to Him, so that Israel is gathered to Him..."*it is too small a thing that You should be My Servant to raise up the tribes of Jacob, and to restore the preserved ones of Israel; I will also give You as a <u>light to the Gentiles</u>, that You should be My salvation to the ends of the earth.*" Isaiah 49:5-6

A Revolutionary Revelation in Jaffa

The first century Messianic community was protective in the same way that the rest of the Jewish community was protective. Along with their contemporaries, the Jewish disciples had been taught from Scripture and had been raised to believe that when Israel got close to Gentiles, they would tend to adopt the idolatrous ways of the Gentiles and fall out of fellowship with God. True. So, to offset that strong training, God sent a supernatural message to Peter while he was on a roof in Joppa (modern day Jaffa, Acts 10:9-17). Getting a confirming visit from Cornelius's delegation at that very moment, he traveled to Caesarea. There, for the first time in the Apostle's illustrious history, he entered a Gentile house and preached Yeshua to a Gentile group. They not only received the message in their hearts and were born from above, but they were also filled with the same Spirit as Peter and the rest of the Messianic Jewish believers. For the remainder of the Book of Acts, we hear of Gentiles who are similarly touched, and enter into the community of faith.

We are the inheritors of that 1st century Acts community. In its opening lines (Acts 1:8) Yeshua gives us our purpose: to be filled with His Spirit and to be witnesses to all the earth. This is the purpose of the Holy Spirit's power, to carry His deliverance to every people group. He had told the disciples earlier:

This Gospel of the kingdom will be preached in <u>all the world</u>...and then the end will come. Matthew 24:14

Yeshua carried God's heart for the whole earth. He was consumed with the heart of the Father as expressed in Isaiah 52:10. *"All the ends of the earth shall see the salvation of our God."*

Also the sons of the foreigner who join themselves to the Lord, to serve Him, and to love the name of the Lord, to be His servants—everyone who keeps from defiling the Sabbath, and holds fast my covenant—even them I will bring to my holy mountain, and make them joyful in my house of prayer. Their burnt offerings and their sacrifices will be accepted on my altar; for my house shall be called a house of prayer for all nations. Isaiah 56:6-7

This has always been God's intention. He distinctly and succinctly revealed His plan through the Hebrew Scriptures, long before the New Testament was even written. This can be seen in the full *TaNaKh* (the acronym used for the Hebrew Scriptures, by combining the first letters of *Torah*—the first Five Books, *Neviim*—the Prophets, and *Khtuvim*—the Writings).

Torah: *"As I live, all the earth will be filled with the glory of the LORD."* Numbers 14:21

Neviim: *"The earth shall be full of the knowledge of the LORD as the waters cover the sea."* Isaiah 11:9

Khtuvim: *"All nations whom you have made shall come and worship before you."* Psalm 86:9

Bringing redemption to the world is not an afterthought. It's not as if God said "Well, the Jews are stubborn, so let's give the opportunity to everybody else and forget plan A." From the beginning, God's intent has been to bring heaven to all the earth. And it's been Israel's calling! In the next chapter I'd like to explore this role more fully.

So the key question is "Who is this God who lives in us by His Spirit? What is the real extent of His concern for humanity? Am I OK not to care for the nations?" Apparently it's not OK, as He made abundantly clear to Peter on that roof in Jaffa. Do the Gentiles only get the leftovers while God's primary focus is on Israel as the "Chosen?"

It's true that Israel has been chosen by God. That's exactly the point. Israel is chosen to be His servant nation, <u>to introduce all other nations to our God</u>. It is Israel's privilege to receive *"the adoption, the glory, the covenants, the giving of the law, the service of God and the promises"* in order to make them real and accessible to all mankind (Romans 9:4). As part of our very essence as a people appointed by God, we are called to bring salvation to the world. Yes, He is the God of Abraham, Isaac and Jacob, but He is also the Father of all mankind. It is vital to grasp that this is His heart…for every tribe and nation.

We don't really know who He is without this aspect of His being. We, the Jewish people, have been entrusted with the riches of His grace. He has raised us from the dead. And He wants to put this same heart in us, His children, His representatives.

So what? So how are we, the Messianic Jews, to walk this out, this calling to be a servant people among the nations? Here are some suggestions for all of us who are the "Solomons" in this comparison:

1. BEFRIENDING His children from the nations…whether they show up here in Israel, or we go there. His heart is expressed as we make even one friend who comes from another nation. Then we encourage them to know us and they can begin to pray for us, and of course we can pray for them too. It happens as we encounter people in Israel from the nations. We become a light to them.

2. SENDING/GOING out from Israel (even to visit family) as Messengers/Ambassadors. Yeshua said *"As the Father sent me, so I send you"* (John 20:21).

3. GIVING a portion of our offerings to bless the nations. Seeing ourselves as those who BLESS not only as those who expect others to bless us.

"This is fine," you may say. We know that Jesus arose within Israel, as the ultimate High Priest, to redeem both Jews and Gentiles. That fulfills Israel's calling, to bring salvation to the world. But what about the Gentiles? How are Yeshua's non-Jewish disciples around the world to express the universality of His heart? "What about us?" As referenced earlier from Romans 11, having received redemption through the Jewish people, the Gentiles (wild olive branches) are now to assist the natural branches in being grafted back in to the Olive Tree.

Midwife to Israel's Rebirth

My oldest daughter's first child was born after an incredible thirty six hours of labor. She went through five midwives. Here's what she said afterward: "I don't see how I could have done it without them, especially the last one. She knew just what I was experiencing and just what to say to encourage and strengthen me to get through the ordeal, birth the child, and become a joyful mom."

I have personally experienced this Gentile role of the "midwife" assisting in the spiritual rebirth of Israel. I was led to the Messiah by Gentiles. We were living way up in the mountains of northern New Mexico when these two young guys, John Nilan and Chris Petroff, showed up. I'm not sure if they knew that my commune partner Russell Resnik and I were Jewish, but they conveyed the love of Yeshua and the reality of His life so unaffectedly that we received them and their message and were "born again" on the spot.

I was first discipled and trained for ministry by Gentiles. My mentor and the director of the evening Bible school I attended was as Gentile as they come. Raised by an Assemblies of God dad and a Nazarene mom, Don Compton was an Anglo-Saxon, Pentecostal Christian through and through. By the grace of God, he had been directed by the Spirit to "work with the hippies" in Santa Fe, New Mexico. The fact is that he was one of the first, back in the 70's, to support me in discovering my Jewish identity and completely backed our initial awkward efforts to celebrate the biblical holidays and bring Jewish people to know Yeshua as Israel's Messiah!

When a Jewish person experiences the miracle of spiritual birth, he is immediately united with all true followers of Yeshua. That brotherhood is the one I was always looking for. It is a brotherhood I've experienced by the simple act of enjoying a meal with Japanese hosts. It is the oneness that releases an anointing that breaks through many long-standing spiritual barriers, as I discovered when I anointed a Korean believer with oil. It is the shared heart of brokenness for Israel's current lost condition and for Europe's past that led me to mingle intercessory tears with a dear German elder on the soil of Deutschland (Germany). You will read of these life-influencing encounters in the pages to come.

Such deep, redemptive Jewish-Gentile friendship has striking precedents in the Scriptures. It is this key that can unlock the mystery of our shared calling—to bring King Messiah back to rule and reign over all the earth. We turn now to more fully investigate Israel's calling to save the world.

Chapter Three

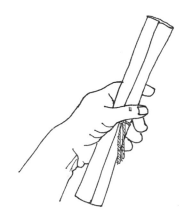

A Messenger People

God's Assignment to Israel is to Bring His Salvation to the World

I will set up a seed after you, who will come from your body, and I will establish his kingdom. He shall build a house for my name, and I will establish the throne of his kingdom forever. I will be his Father, and he shall be my son. 2 Samuel 7:12-14a

Your throne, O God, is forever and ever; a scepter of righteousness is the scepter of your kingdom...Therefore God, your God, has anointed you with the oil of gladness more than your companions. Psalm 45:6-7

For unto us a child is born, unto us a son is given; and the government shall be upon his shoulder. And his name shall be called Wonderful, Counselor, Mighty God, Everlasting Father, Prince of Peace. Of the increase of his government and peace there will be no end. Upon the throne of David and over his kingdom... Isaiah 9:6-7

When they came to put us in the police wagon we didn't resist. That morning a sober sense of purpose propelled us to put our bodies in the doorway of the U.S. Army Induction Center in Oakland, California. It was December, 1967 and we felt an urgency about shutting down the military machine that was bringing death to Vietnamese and American soldiers alike. As the result of our "caper" we sat in jail for twenty-one days. Our immediate circle of radicals included a disproportionate number of young Jews.

The same was true of the "back to the land" movement that began in that era, after our disillusionment with political protest. As a searching nineteen year old, I was taken to a snow-surrounded shack in upstate New York where twenty-five or so hippies were tasting the early days of experimental communal existence. Amidst crying babies, a huge pot of brown rice and a pot-bellied stove in the center of the ramshackle room, we dreamed of a total alternative to modern society, a society that no longer seemed relevant. We dreamed of being completely free from the industrial-technological world around us. Cooperative agriculture, shared resources, organic life cycle celebration and tribal lifestyle were all high values for us. These were goals we were ready to sacrifice for. Our fellow pioneers had Jewish family names like Prensky, Hoffman, Kaymen, Landau and Cohen. We were seekers and revolutionaries by nature.

Why? Why are the Jewish people drawn to social change, radical movements and spiritual alternatives? What's the connection with King Solomon and the Lord's decision to build His Temple in Jerusalem, Israel, some 3,000 years ago? It's because God gave us the assignment to bring world redemption. I'm not exaggerating. It all began with father Abraham.

Here are some of the many serious statements God makes to Jewish people in His book regarding the "mission" of Israel. We've seen some of them already, but I repeat them here for emphasis.

- *"In your seed all the nations of the earth will be blessed."* Genesis 22:18
- *"You shall be to me a kingdom of priests and a holy nation."* Exodus 19:6
- *"My house* [the Temple Solomon and Hiram built] *shall be called a house of prayer for all nations."* Isaiah 56:7
- *"...you shall receive power when the Holy Spirit has come upon you and you shall be witnesses to me in Jerusalem, and in all Judea and Samaria, and to the end of the earth."* Acts 1:8

From cover to cover the Scriptures affirm this as Israel's original calling—to bring the knowledge of God to all nations. We can try to dodge it. We can attempt to deny it. But we can't escape it. And neither can serious Bible students sidestep this profound truth. This is not to say that there will be no Gentile messengers. The symbolism of Hiram and Solomon collaborating to build the Temple reflects God's intention to involve the Gentiles, too. If there were no Gentile messengers, few of us Jewish believers would have found Yeshua. Yet to have a healthy understanding of our relationship with each other there must be recognition of our God-given role in history. The Jewish Redeemer, Yeshua, is the ultimate expression of this "worldwide mission."

It is too small a thing that you should be my servant to raise up the tribes of Jacob, and to restore the preserved ones of Israel; I will also give you as a light to the Gentiles that you should be my salvation [yeshua-ti in Hebrew] to the ends of the earth. Isaiah 49:6

We must embrace both Israel's calling as a priestly "firstborn" nation, providing atonement for all nations and the equally loved status of every people and tribe. Then we find the heart of God, the Father of all mankind. For me this has special significance. In my days of searching for the truth that would transform the world, we were exposed to several answers, but each one was exclusive and most were only relevant for a select group of seekers. Let me explain.

Lotus Position and Stacks of Books

Some claimed that you had to sit in a full lotus position (legs crossed one on top of the other, forming a painful pretzel for all but the most limber), spending long hours meditating to achieve enlightenment. This excluded me and most other normally constructed human beings. Others gave you a tall stack of books to read, claiming that salvation lay in comprehending complex philosophical equations of reality. But then only the most intellectual individual had a chance. Another path we diligently attempted was to divorce ourselves from the normal world and live an ascetic life of material denial, taking monk-like vows. This not only disqualified the vast portion of earth's population, it failed to bring global transformation. None of these paths were universally available to everyone on the planet.

I love it that God tells us in so many places in the Hebrew Scriptures that His plan includes all races and tribes:

As I live, all the earth shall be filled with the glory of the Lord. Numbers 14:21

All the earth shall worship you and sing praises to you... Psalm 66:4

Oh let the nations be glad and sing for joy! For you shall...govern the nations on earth. Psalm 67:4

God shall bless us and all the ends of the earth shall fear Him. Psalm 67:7

All nations whom you have made shall come and worship before you. Psalm 86:9

For the earth shall be full of the knowledge of the LORD as the waters cover the sea. Isaiah 11:9

For the Gentiles shall seek Him… Isaiah 11:10

He will set up a banner for the nations and will assemble the outcasts of Israel. Isaiah 11:12

Who would not fear you, O King of the nations? Jeremiah 10:7

The Gentiles shall come to you [Israel's God!] *from the ends of the earth…* Jeremiah 16:19

The origin of Solomon's mandate to build the Temple can be seen all the way back in God's announcement to Abraham in their first recorded conversation. *"Through your seed all the nations of the earth will be blessed"* (Genesis 12:3). God declared, for all history to take notice, that through this man all the nations of the earth would be blessed. His subsequent name change from Abram (Father is lofty) to Abraham (Father of a multitude, or many nations) proclaims his prophetic calling to bring salvation to the whole world. God's heart was not just for one family. Four thousand years ago God wanted to save the whole world. Abraham's willingness to sacrifice his son inspired God to make a profound promise. *"Because you have done this thing, and have not withheld your son, your only son…In your seed all the nations of the earth shall be blessed"* (Genesis 22:16, 18).

The Jewish Mission is World Redemption

The Gentiles are all the nations of the world beyond Israel. Their path to God is directly and solely through the Seed of Abraham, the Messiah. In other words, the Jewish mission is world redemption. This mission can be seen from the time of the Patriarchs. Joseph, a great grandson of Abraham, interceded on behalf of mankind during a famine that covered the neighboring lands. All the surrounding countries came to Joseph to buy grain. In this way, Joseph was a predecessor of the Messiah. Through Joseph, not just the family of his father Jacob, but a multitude of nations was saved from death. A few generations later Moses arrived on the scene. And, of course, Moses was also a type of Yeshua. He brought Israel out of Egypt, by the blood of each household's lamb, and into Israel's inheritance. On Mt. Sinai God revealed Israel's priestly role (Exodus 19:4-6, cited in Chapter 2). Israel was to provide reconciliation between a holy God and a sinful world. This was ultimately achieved by Messiah Yeshua's high priestly sacrifice.

Solomon was the son of David, a direct descendant of Abraham. The Lord made a covenant with David promising him an everlasting kingdom and a Son who would sit on the throne forever. Therefore, Solomon's full calling included world redemption. He could not build the Temple alone, because the Temple needed to (a) reflect the shared kingdom destiny of Jew and Gentile in its construction by both Solomon and Hiram and (b) begin to open the doors to the salvation of all tribes and peoples, as indicated in Solomon's dedication prayer (1 Kings 8:43).

It helps to review a timeless account of Yeshua's mission to the world. One of the New Testament writers, Luke, reports Zachariah's prophecy in the Gospel of Luke 1:68-69. *"Blessed is the Lord God of Israel, for He has visited and redeemed His people, and has raised up a horn of salvation for us in the house of His servant David."* Yeshua told the woman at the well *"salvation is of the Jews"* (John 4:22). The clear teaching of Scripture is that Israel will be used to bring the nations (Gentiles, *goyim*) to the saving knowledge of the God of Abraham. This, however, sets up a potential cause of jealousy/resentment. "Hey, Lord! Why them and not me? I'm special too, aren't I?"

The answer lies in a humble acceptance of God's right to select nations, tribes, or individuals to accomplish His purposes. Some of us are women and some are men. We can argue with that designation and claim that it's a mistake, but it does little good. We did not choose, nor can we change our gender. Israel's chosen role creates a vital starting point for the end-time partnership of Hiram (Christians) and Solomon (Messianic Jews). Yet the embrace of Israel's special role in history must be free from self-denigration or the unscriptural conclusion that Jews are "better." As Deuteronomy 7:7 states, *"The Lord did not set His love on you nor choose you because you were more in number than any other people, for you were the least of all peoples."*

I am especially fond of Daniel Gruber's formulation of this truth:

In repeating these things to Jacob (the commandment to *"Be fruitful and multiply"* as an extension of the commandment initially given to Adam), God was signifying that His original plan for the earth was still in effect, and that Jacob and the people that would come from him were the means of bringing it to fulfillment. For that purpose, God established a covenant relationship with Israel—with Israel only of all the peoples of the earth. *"You only have I known of all the families of the earth..."* (Amos 3:2). Israel was to be God's key for unlocking the nations, setting them free, and bringing them back to Himself. God was not abandoning all the other families of the earth to futility and destruction. He was simply affirming the means He had chosen for their redemption—Noah, Abraham, Isaac, and Jacob. The earth was still for Man, and God had chosen Abraham to be the "heir of the world" (cf. Romans 4:13). God was expressing His intent to restore the earth to its original purpose.[3]

Another question we must answer is "What will bring real peace to this tortured world?" This was the question that troubled us during our protest in the doorway of the United States Army Induction Center in late 1967 and later, when we were organic hippie farmers in the wilds of the New Mexico mountains. "Is there a God? Does He care about human beings? What is the destiny of this world?" We were so shocked to discover that the Bible addresses these and every other vital question. The Lord's rooftop message to Peter in Acts 10 was, "Yes, you must not discount those who are different. I have raised up the Messiah for every tribe and nation."

People are now noticing that there is something special about Israel. Does that mean that His sole focus is on world Jewry and that the Gentiles get the leftovers? Not at all. Israel is indeed His servant nation. We have been privileged to receive the revelations of God and the responsibility to preserve His commandments. Yet, Israel's calling is for the benefit of all tribes and people groups.

It is impossible to know God without knowing Him in both of these contexts—as the God of Abraham, Isaac and Israel and as the Father of all mankind. This is His heart. We have been entrusted with the riches of His grace, for the Jew and also for the Gentile (Romans 1:16). We have been drawn into a most unexpected covenant with our Maker, through His Son. This covenant requires that we respect God's choice of vessel and that we honor His all-inclusiveness too. It is a covenant relationship between Jews and Gentiles. The New Testament calls it a mystery. In the following chapter we will look into the Lord's genius in fashioning us as two and yet one.

Chapter Four

God's Mystery Thriller

The Gentiles' Surprise Role in Israel's Salvation

...that through the mercy shown you they [Israel] *also may also obtain mercy.*
Romans 11:31b

Then Hiram gave Solomon cedar and cypress logs according to all his desire.
1 Kings 5:10

T he flight from Hong Kong to Osaka found me tired, but unable to sleep. With a personal movie screen embedded in the seat in front of me, what was I to do, but surf through the inexhaustible film options available? I chose a mystery based on an unsolved series of murder cases in 1960s San Francisco.

I got pretty involved in the intricate story line, and as the actors finally closed in on the villain I was really looking forward to the solution. Right then the pilot's voice broke into the movie. "We will now be starting our final descent. That will conclude our entertainment program on this flight." I almost protested out loud. "Oh no! Now I'll have to find a copy of that film. I've gotta find out how it ends."

The Mystery: Israel's Salvation and Gentiles as Fellow Heirs

When I reached Osaka for an Asian conference on Israel and Messianic Jews, it hit me. The intrigue of a well-told mystery is just what God meant when He used that word to refer to the enigma of Jews and Gentiles being one in Messiah. Speaking to believers in Rome, Paul says:

I do not desire, brethren, that you should be ignorant of this mystery…blindness in part has happened to Israel until the fullness of the Gentiles has come in. And so all Israel will be saved… Romans 11:25-26

Again, writing to the Ephesians he says that God showed him by revelation,

…the mystery of Messiah, which in other ages was not made known to the sons of men…that the Gentiles should be fellow heirs (with the Jewish disciples), *of the same body…* Ephesians 3:4-6

From the perspective of history, there is no logic that brings together Jewish and Gentile people. Thus, knowing in advance what would happen, the Lord speaks to the Apostle and uses the word that clearly indicates an unusual, unexpected, inexplicable event. In Greek, *musterion* indicates something that has been hidden but is now revealed. In his communication with both the Romans and the Ephesians, Paul makes it clear by using the term *musterion* that this shared destiny seems plenty strange and challenging for his readers to grasp. Truly, it takes a lot of humility. But isn't that just where the Lord wants to take us?

As I arrived in Osaka and the Japanese-initiated event unfolded, two things were strikingly evident. First, there was a refreshing harmony of numerous church leaders who previously had not been so enthused to associate with each other (their description). And second, there was a yearning to understand and serve God's purposes for Asia and Israel together with us, their Israeli Messianic Jewish brothers. I was watching the "solution" to God's mystery thriller: "How will Israel be saved and the Gentiles become true fellow heirs?" It thrilled us all.

A Mystery Solved

After two wonderfully intense conferences in Osaka and Tokyo, plus a very full weekend of ministry, I took the return flight to Hong Kong. As I had hoped, the same mystery movie was available for viewing. Eager to see the end of the mystery, I opened the little screen and scrolled to the last scene I remembered. This time I got to see the ending. And though I'm not going to tell you how the movie ends, I'm delighted to be involved in the real-life mystery we are engaged in together.

The more I learn of this mystery, the more thrilling it is. We are experiencing the long-promised release of love's resources coming toward Israel in waves (Isaiah 60:5). At a time when many are clamoring for Israel's punishment and rejection, it brings us bright hope, added courage, and needed comfort to know that our Gentile family members are activated on behalf of their Israeli Messianic brothers and sisters.

In the previous chapter I highlighted Israel's calling to bring salvation to all nations. Now, in a case of true poetic justice, it becomes the role of the Gentiles to return the favor. This, the Apostle Paul makes abundantly clear in Romans 11:11-12. He admits that the Jewish people seem to have been cast aside by God, but bounces back with these strong words:

I say then, have they stumbled that they should fall? Certainly not! But through their fall, to provoke them to jealousy, salvation has come to the Gentiles. Now if their fall is riches for the world, and their failure riches for the Gentiles, how much more their fullness.

Many of Yeshua's Israeli disciples were bothered by the entrance of the Gentiles. Earlier, I referred to the dramatic vision that Peter needed to receive on the Jaffa roof before he would give the Good News to Cornelius, a Roman officer, and his group of non-Jews waiting up the coast in Caesarea. The ensuing influx of non-Jewish believers changed the complexion of the kingdom forever.[4] Yet there was a prophetic element to the way God opened the Apostles' hearts to receive the Gentiles. The Book of Acts begins with the celebration of Pentecost (the Feast of Weeks or *Shavuot* in Hebrew), when two loaves of leavened bread are waved as an offering unto God, as the Torah requires. I believe that because these two loaves are leavened (and thus symbolize a dimension of impurity) they cannot represent the Messiah. Rather, the two loaves are a divine way of demonstrating Jews and Gentiles as one before God.

In fact, in a fascinating way the rhythm of the biblical feasts explains history. The entrance of non-Jews into the Messiah's redemption signals what could be called the age of the Gentiles. The alignment of the seven feasts originally given to Israel and their fulfillment in Yeshua, places a unique emphasis on the past two millenia. Each feast must find its fulfillment in Yeshua. God continually brings us back to Him. And thus it is with this feast.

The In-Between Feast that Sheds Light on the Mystery

Shavuot (the Feast of Weeks) is a unique festival, standing between Passover and the Feast of Tabernacles, amidst the three pilgrim feasts. The first, Passover (in the spring), tells the story of our salvation. It represents the first coming of the Lord—how He was the Lamb of God that took away the sin of the world. Through a lamb's blood the Israelites were freed from Egyptian slavery and through Yeshua's blood we are all likewise freed from the universal slavery of sin. Prophetically and historically, Passover culminates in Yeshua's sacrifice and resurrection, bringing us to the Feast of First Fruits (Leviticus 23:10-11). In the spring we celebrate a cluster of three feasts: Passover, Unleavened Bread and First Fruits. This cluster represents Yeshua's life, atoning death and resurrection.

Skipping to the fall, we have the Feast of Trumpets (aka *Rosh Ha-Shana*), the Day of Atonement (*Yom Kippur*) and the Feast of Tabernacles (*Sukkot*). This climactic sequence of celebrations features the *shofar* (a prominent symbol of the Messiah's second coming), a day to repent and recognize our need for the atonement of sin, and finally the feast of *Sukkot*, said to represent the ultimate in-gathering of all nations to worship the King. (Zechariah 14 describes this uniting of the nations under Israel's King.)

But, what about *Shavuot*, the Feast of Weeks? This "middle" feast is only one day. Yet it is a harvest feast and has prominence in well-established Jewish tradition as the timing of Moses receiving the tablets of the law on Mt. Sinai. As mentioned, it was also the feast God chose to pour out His Spirit on Yeshua's disciples in Acts 2.

So, if the spring feasts represent Messiah's first coming, and the fall feasts His return and ultimate reign over the earth, where is He found in the symbolism of *Shavuot*? Interestingly, He vacates the scene just days before the Feast of Weeks arrives. The timing of this feast is seven full weeks after Passover. Prior to Yeshua's departure, He promises His Spirit, gives instructions for His absence, and takes off without a trace! Not only that, but within a few decades the Temple is destroyed (again!) and Israel is cast out of the land, into an exile of nearly 2,000 years. Of this Hosea writes in Chapter 3:4-5, noting that Israel will endure many years without royalty or priesthood, but that we will finally seek God and David our King. This, by the way, is a stunning prophecy of Israel's end-time revival and recognition of Yeshua, David's greater Son, concurrent with our return to the land.

It must be that we are the fulfillment of Yeshua's prophetic presence in the Feast of Weeks, *Shavuot*. Fittingly, the Book of Acts is written about the outworking of the faith, through Yeshua's disciples, following His departure. He lived through them and He lives through us. He has been living through every one faithful to His name for the past twenty centuries. *Shavuot* represents the age of the believers in the earth, between the first and second comings.

Not only are the Gentiles "let in" during the early years of faith, at the beginning of this age, but their leadership becomes the focal point of those following Yeshua, who is now called by His Greek name *Yesous*, or Jesus. After the Jews are expelled from their land, the Church Age begins. Yeshua is no longer physically, personally present as a man on earth. So, to repeat, if all the feasts are fulfilled in Him, He must also be seen during this age. And He is seen. He is visible in us, in the believers. His earthly "address" is the collective presence of all who follow Him, both Jew and Gentile. We have received His commission… to bring to the earth His ministry, His presence. He told us to make disciples of all men.

In Yeshua's last words of instructions to His disciples He gave the plan for this age.

All authority has been given to Me in heaven and on earth. [By this authority I'm commissioning you to do what's most important.] *Go therefore and make disciples of all the nations, immersing them in the name of the Father and the Son and of the Holy Spirit, teaching them to observe all things that I have commanded you; and lo, I am with you always, even to the end of the age.* Matthew 28:18-20

Yeshua defines the main activity, making disciples, then assures us that He will be with us as we do it, during this entire age! In the defining text of Act 1:4-8, Yeshua is asked by His disciples *"Will You at this time restore the kingdom?"* Will Israel return to her glory? The Master says:

It is not for you to know...but you shall receive power when the Holy Spirit has come upon you; and you shall be witnesses to me in Jerusalem, and in all Judea and Samaria, and to the end of the earth. Acts 1:7-8

In other words, NO, that's not what this period of time is about. Israel will only be restored after you complete your witness to Jerusalem, Judea, Samaria and the uttermost parts of the earth.

The unmistakable and radical shift in Acts corresponds both to Yeshua's "absence" from the earth and the joining of the nations to Israel in embracing the King. Only when we, the congregation of Yeshua in the earth, Jew and Gentile, have completed the task given to us by the Messiah, Lamb and Lion, Sacrifice and Sovereign...will we see Him coming in the clouds of glory, riding a white horse as the King of Kings and the Lord of Lords.

I believe in the restoration of apostolic faith in Israel, and in the earth in our time. But what does it mean to be apostolic? Are we to put the emphasis on individual leaders or on a way of life? My understanding is that the Spirit is calling us to return to a way of life—to the radicalism and simplicity of the first century. This is relevant to the issue of the "age of *Shavuot*," because we are called to manifest His restoration together. At last, the Jewish people are returning to the place of closeness to our God and to serving the nations, as was originally intended. An apostolic view of the world must, by definition, carry a burden for the salvation of every nation. This is our job, together, as Messiah's interceding disciples.

Shavuot is Messiah dwelling in the gathering of His people. His presence is manifest when we are worshiping Him, when we are praying, when we are in His word, when we are responding to His delegated authority in men, when we are witnessing, when we are being filled with His Spirit, when we break bread. This is the design and pleasure of God in this age. This brings so much glory to God, to Yeshua's name. The mystery of *Shavuot* is that it points to Yeshua both when He is in heaven, seated at the right hand of the Father, and at the same time on earth—through the body of His followers, inhabited by His Spirit.

An Unlikely Match

The Book of Acts later unfolds the first-time scenario of God supernaturally authoring the previously forbidden joint fellowship of His followers. The Jewish Apostles must convene a special council in Jerusalem (Acts 15) to deal with this new situation. Their decision was to open the door to the other nations, that they could become followers of Yeshua without converting to Judaism. Radical.

Interestingly, the question today is precisely the opposite. Can Jews embrace Jesus without converting to Christianity? This question is highly absurd in light of the debate that raged in the first century. After nearly twenty centuries, however, the combination of Church anti-Semitism and the dominant Gentile culture of those worshiping Him, has given a lot of weight to this question.

We are seeing a fascinating reversal of excruciating centuries of negative reaction by the Church to the Jews, as God draws His international followers toward their formerly estranged Jewish brethren. It was these very brethren, at the outset, who opened the door for them. Isn't it only fair that now they open the door to the House of Jacob? The original recipients of the Gospel have long been blocked from entering the kingdom that was once their sole possession! I think this "turn-around" is exactly what God has in mind. That's why I would like to use this book to encourage our dedicated non-Jewish brethren in Yeshua to "give Him back to us" as part of this "putting all things in order" that is expressed by the traditional Hebrew term *tikkun*. A *tikkun* in modern Hebrew is a repair. The traditional concept carries the "repair" or the "restoration" of the entire world to its original, God-intended form. Only Yeshua can do that. Only Yeshua can reverse the damage done by history. He got separated from His natural family and Scriptural/cultural roots in the process of widening salvation to include all mankind. This all-inclusiveness is apropos. As we have stated in Chapter 2, His mission was worldwide. However, there now needs to be a course correction. A big one. It's time for Yeshua's own Jewish people to rejoice in the gift of salvation provided by our gracious God, the God of Israel.

Two thousand years later the spiritual roles have, at least in part, been reversed. Now it is the Gentile believers who have the numerical prominence and the tools. Now is the Church's hour of opportunity to render recognition and assistance to the works being established among the sons of Jacob. I call it the "Hiram Factor." Hiram, the King of Tyre, served the purposes of the King of Israel and found his own reward therein. His role in building the Temple was a key. "Hiram" (the Gentiles) is now holding the same key.

There is something so pleasing to God and so puzzling to Jewish people when Gentiles turn toward us, not with anti-Semitic judgment, but with respect and appreciation. The point of Hiram and Solomon's story is that their relationship does not stop there. Theirs is a covenant bond. They were initially drawn together through their mutual love for King David. But now, in the verses at the beginning of the chapter, Hiram expresses great joy to be digging into God's construction project with Solomon. Establishing a house for God's glory in Jerusalem gives concrete expression to their connection. Solomon, the Jew, embraced Hiram, the Gentile. Similarly, the first century saw Jesus' Jewish followers embrace the Gentiles as equals in the faith. How appropriate that, like Hiram, the nations should now turn, in gratitude, to partner with Solomon, their Messianic Jewish brothers.

In return for Hiram's participation, Solomon was eager to share the bounty of his land. He was not willing to do all the receiving. He made a commitment to send wheat and oil to Hiram. Blessings were poured out upon Hiram as an immediate result of his part in building the Temple. Here there is a vivid picture of the harvest (wheat) and the anointing (oil) that God wants to release for each Christian who takes part in Israel's rebirth. This heaven-sent release of God's grace and power is the subject of our next chapter.

Chapter Five

Where the Anointing Oil Flows

Natural and Wild Olive Branches Dwelling Securely Change History

And Solomon gave Hiram twenty thousand kors of wheat as food for his household and twenty kors of pressed oil. So the Lord gave Solomon wisdom as He had promised him; and there was peace between Hiram and Solomon and the two of them made a covenant together. 1 Kings 5:11-12

Standing in Seoul, Korea at the end of my first journey there, I was approached by a Korean woman whom I knew to be a dedicated intercessor for Israel. She asked me to pray for her, which I did, placing a single drop of olive oil in the palm of her hand. A strong, sweet anointing was released and the following thought flooded in upon me, generated from Romans 11. "When the natural branches and the wild branches become one in the ancient root, the oil of God's anointed presence flows. When the wild branches (Gentile believers) embrace both the Jewish roots of their faith in Messiah and their covenant Jewish brothers who have reconnected with those roots through Yeshua, the oil flows. And when the natural branches (Jewish believers in Yeshua) rejoice without protective fear, knowing that the wild branches belong—

THIS releases the olive oil. From the one olive tree, all branches to-gether, will flow freely the oil of His anointing to break the yoke off of our people Israel."

Jealousy and envy are the enemies of God's presence. Our natu-ral tendency is to compare ourselves with others and measure whether we have as much as they do. Am I being honored as much? Is my importance recognized as I feel it should be? In our day, the Body of Messiah is finally rediscovering her Jewish roots. This is a phenomenal and welcome change. Yet it brings with it the temptation for Gentiles to feel inferior and Jews to feel superior. It can also threaten Messianic Jews, who sometimes feel overwhelmed by the sheer volume of Gen-tile Christian interest in "Jewish roots" and Israel. On the other hand, the same Gentiles can react with hurt and resentment when their en-thusiasm is misunderstood. Still others become passionately political "Christian Zionists" and fail to relate with Messianic Jews at all. Olive oil in a Korean hand helped me to comprehend God's solution to these unnecessary and unhealthy overreactions.

When Gentile believers embrace both the Jewish roots of their faith in Messiah and their covenant Jewish brothers, without trying to become Jewish—the oil flows. When Jewish believers rejoice, secure in the knowledge of their identity and openly accepting the wild olive branches as their brothers in the New Covenant, the oil flows. From the one olive tree, when all the branches are secure in their relationship with one another and their worth in the Lord, the oil flows.

There is a human, personal ingredient here worth noting. It has to do with our openness to each other. At our facility in Israel, we receive a large number of visitors from the nations. This is a great blessing. At the same time it calls for an open heart, to approach each new person with appreciation and respect for the effort they've made to come to Is-rael and to find us, since we are located way off the beaten track, on the back side of a small and virtually unknown industrial area. In fact, let me take this opportunity to apologize to the many intrepid visitors who have set out to find us, only to arrive closer to the end of our worship service than the beginning, because they couldn't find the place.

Being open to one another means demonstrating mutual respect, recognizing the place of value each holds in God's plan. We both have something to give and something to receive. Hiram sent Solomon timber and workers. Solomon sent Hiram wheat and oil. It is in the exchange that we discover the Lord's grace and our fulfillment in the calling He gave us. It is not in trying to be identical with each other.

Was anyone called while circumcised? Let him not be uncircumcised. Was anyone called while uncircumcised? Let him not be circumcised. 1 Corinthians 7:18

In the first century, circumcision was understood not only as a physical condition, but as a declaration of commitment to the way of life given to Israel in the Torah. The same author, Paul the Apostle, adds when writing to the Galatians:

For in Messiah Yeshua neither circumcision nor uncircumcision avails anything, but faith working through love. Galatians 5:6

It fascinates me that God is using the re-emergence of the Messianic Jewish community to force both Jewish and Gentile disciples of Yeshua to a place of humility and mutual recognition. The raw fact is that we need each other. Yeshua will not return until He hears His Jewish followers in sufficient numbers say, *"Blessed is He who comes in the name of the Lord"* (Matthew 23:39). Neither will He return until His Gentile followers welcome the natural branches back into the tree from which we were broken off.

For I speak to you Gentiles; inasmuch as I am an apostle to the Gentiles, I magnify my ministry if by any means I may provoke to jealousy those who are my flesh and save some of them. For if their being cast away is the reconciling of the world, what will their acceptance be but life from the dead. Romans 11:13-15

For if you were cut out of the olive tree which is wild by nature, and were grafted contrary to nature into a cultivated olive tree, how much more will these, who are natural branches, be grafted into their own olive tree. Romans 11:24

There is another intriguing use of the olive tree found in the Hebrew Scriptures. In Chapter 4 of the Book of Zechariah the author asks *"What are these two olive trees—at the right of the lampstand and at its left"* (Zechariah 4:11)? He sees that there are two olive branches that both drip into gold pipes. The oil that flows through these pipes lights all of the seven golden lampstands that constitute the divine word of grace to the prophet and the rebuilding of the Temple (vv.2-10). The entire passage concludes with the angel's revelation that *"These are the two anointed ones who stand beside the Lord of the whole earth"* (Zechariah 4:14). Could this be us—the Jewish and Gentile members of Messiah's Body on earth? Wow! Even the possibility that we could stand beside Yeshua at the end of the age is thrilling.

How can we serve the purposes of God in our generation? That is the driving question behind this book. I want to bring a perspective on the Gentiles' role in our redemption that will encourage them to take their honored place. And I want to assist my Messianic Jewish brethren to see the essential, prophetic place God has for our Gentile brothers and sisters at this time, in our lifetimes. There is, without a doubt, a greater power and anointing that needs to be released in these end times. The darkness is growing. The light must increase to overcome it and to draw those out of darkness who can be rescued. That greater anointing is released when Messianic Jews are secure enough to embrace the Gentiles who are called to labor in our midst, and when Gentile believers are secure enough to know that they do not have to become Jews, nor act like Jews. Romans, Chapter 11, exhorts the non-Jewish disciple to have a right heart toward us. But we also need a right heart toward them.

The extent to which God challenges us to be involved in each other's salvation, is eloquently highlighted by Yeshua, immediately before He departs for heaven. When the Jewish disciples asked about the kingdom being restored to Israel, the King told them:

It is not for you to know the times or seasons which the Father has put in His own authority. But you shall receive power when the Holy Spirit has come upon you; and you shall be witnesses to me in Jerusalem, and in all Judea and Samaria and to the end of the earth. Acts 1:7-8

It's as if He said, "Yes, I want you to announce my Messiahship in Jerusalem. But don't stop there. I'm burdened for the Gentiles in Samaria that don't seem connected with you, and all the way to the last tribe existing on the face of the earth. Tell every one of them too."

My heart has been deepened to experience this aspect of the Lord's viewpoint in many parts of the world. But it never happened more than when I was in Japan.

The Heart of God for Japan

Sitting cross-legged on the matted floor of a traditional Japanese home, I looked out the window at a simple but vibrant garden. My hosts, Takeo Muraoka and his wife, Tomoko, had spread before me a feast of perfectly prepared, delicately served vegetables, tofu, rice, tender beef and green tea. With chopsticks in hand, I ate and talked at an unusually restful and satisfying pace. It seemed that I had entered a very different, and much more civilized "time zone."

Japan was eye-opening and compassion-stirring. While humbled and deeply edified by the refined, artistic way of life in Japan—I was also grieved by the high incidence of suicide that requires barriers to block passengers from leaping in front of moving trains. On the one hand there is an attention to beauty, power and elegance in visual design, and on the other, there is a desperation and dissatisfaction in the Japanese soul that leads to death.

Hearing God's broken heart for the Japanese people, I found myself calling the believers in Tokyo and Osaka to *"look on the fields that are already ripe for harvest."* Many earnest and dedicated servants of God there asked, "How can I further the salvation of Israel?" I was privileged to speak about this from the prophets, especially Isaiah's statement that *"the sons of foreigners will build up your walls."* Yet covenant friendship is reciprocal. The salvation of Israel is not all God is concerned about. He wants *"all men to be saved and to come to the knowledge of the truth"* (1 Timothy 2:4). Simeon declares in Luke 2:32, in a defining reference to Isaiah 42:6 and 49:6, that Yeshua will be:

A light to bring revelation to the Gentiles, and the glory of your people, Israel.

In the next chapter (Luke 3:4, 6), John the Immerser quotes the prophet Isaiah again, emphasizing that this Messiah will *"prepare the way of the Lord"* and that through Him *"all flesh will see the salvation of God."* All flesh? That's pretty inclusive. No one is left out. And did you notice the combination in the Lord's formula? The Savior will come to both the Gentiles and to Israel.

We need to pray for the raising up of an indigenous movement of "Japanese-flavored" faith in Yeshua in Japan (and in all other nations) that utilizes the creative forms of expression native to each nation.

Nothing less than *"life from the dead"* is promised when we get this relationship right. Hiram and Solomon got it right. They walked in friendship and shared resources; and they saw the glory of God rest upon the house they built for God. This motivates us to discover our shared calling as interceding priests before God's throne.

Chapter Six

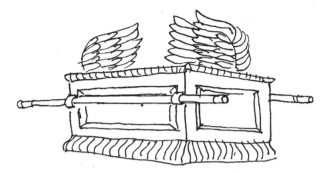

Shared Priesthood

A German and a Jew Before the Throne,
Experience His Glorious Presence

And it came to pass, when the priests came out of the holy place, that the cloud filled the house of the Lord so that the priests could not continue ministering, because of the cloud; for the glory of the Lord filled the house of the Lord.
1 Kings 8:10-11

It took me several seconds to realize what day it was. It was *Yom HaShoah*, Holocaust Remembrance Day. But I was not here in Israel; I was in Germany, the guest of Prince Albrecht Castell. How profound it was to sit with a German man in his 80's, who bears permanent grief for being carried by the Nazi tide, as a young man during the Third Reich. My dignified host suggested that we pray. While praying for the peoples of Germany and Israel, we each began weeping, hardly aware of the other's tears. But as the tears increased we wept in each other's arms, our hearts tenderly united in Yeshua. We ached together under the weight of Germany's role in authoring the slaughter of six million Jews, and—at the same time—the chasm separating Israel and her Messiah. In that heaviness, the scent of His favor drifted by. Was this similar to the "pleasing aroma" referred to when a sacrifice pleased God?

In Israel's ancient history, the role of the priests included the holy task of making blood sacrifices. This in itself was a form of intercession, securing atonement for the sins of repentant Israelites. But their intercessory ministry also included a serious burden in prayer. In Exodus 28:29-30 we have a portrait of the priest who is to enter the Holy of Holies, his breastplate adorned with twelve precious stones representing the twelve tribes of Israel. It was to be worn...

...over Aaron's heart when he goes in before the Lord. So Aaron shall bear the judgment of the children of Israel over his heart before the Lord continually. Exodus 28:30

Not incidentally, the dedication of Solomon and Hiram's Temple was accompanied by the ministry of Israel's priests. But the glory of God infiltrated the occasion and they could not remain standing as they attempted to conduct their sacrificial rituals. The house that a Jew and a Gentile built, in a lasting display of joint obedience to the Most High God, was filled with His glory. This is the glory that will descend upon us as we exercise His priestly calling together. Peter captures this shared calling by quoting Exodus 19:6, spoken over Israel in the original context, and applying it to New Covenant believers.

But you are a chosen generation, a royal priesthood, a holy nation, His own special people, that you may proclaim the praises of Him who called you out of darkness into His marvelous light; who once were not a people but are now the people of God, who had not obtained mercy but now have obtained mercy. 1 Peter 2:9-10

The prophet Joel takes up the intercessory calling of the priests in his latter days' description.

Let the priests who minister to the Lord weep between the porch and the altar, and let them say "Spare your people, O God." Joel 2:17

He goes on to promise the latter rain and the final harvest— remarkable developments in Israel, preparing the way for King Yeshua's arrival. Here, God promises an outpouring in the end times, after Israel returns from exile (Joel 3:1). But first, there must be priestly, tearful intercession:

Then [when the priests have come, weeping] *the Lord will be zealous for His land, and pity His people. The Lord will answer* [those prayers] *and say to His people, "Behold, I will send you grain and new wine and oil* [all symbols of fruitfulness] *and you will be satisfied by them; I will no longer make you a reproach among the nations."* Joel 2:18-19

What stands out here is that Joel sees the priests weeping. He tells them to cry while they are interceding for Israel's redemption. Tears are like a leakage from the heart. We are so constructed that when our emotions are overflowing, we are most likely to shed tears. God's own emotion toward unsaved Israel is on display here. He commands His priestly intercessors to participate in His depth of compassion for the return and revival of His lost people, Israel. As Jewish and Gentile intercessors this is a weighty place. It is just what I experienced with Prince Castell on German soil.

He Who Sows in Tears Shall Reap in Joy

The author of Psalm 126 goes so far as to indicate that tears are a necessary prelude to the joy of the harvest. Could this be one reason we have not yet seen the completion of Israel's spiritual return and our national repentance, when we turn back to the heart of God? There is a clear promise that goes with this weeping as seed is sown.

Those who sow in tears shall reap in joy. He who continually goes forth weeping, bearing seed for sowing, shall doubtless come again with rejoicing, bringing his sheaves with him. Psalm 126:5-6

Known as "the weeping prophet," Jeremiah is both a priest and a prophet. As God shows him how Israel betrayed His initial fatherly promise, the prophet's heart is broken. Finally undone, he moans, in these immortal words:

Oh that my head were waters and my eyes a fountain of tears, that I might weep day and night for the slain of the daughter of my people. Jeremiah 9:1

Talk about adopting the heart of God for His lost people! I can only compare it with birth in the natural realm. Obviously, never having gone through the event myself, I can only go by the accounts of women who've described the experience to me. But one recently said, "I thought my life was going to end. My body was being turned inside out. There is no way to describe how much it hurt." Yet seeing the babe at her breast a few days later, it was evident that her joy now far outweighed the agony she'd gone through. Such delight awaits us, as we embrace the price of being His weeping intercessors, giving birth to a resurrected Israel.

The biblical account of Hannah, crying out, inconsolable in her barrenness, mirrors this anguish. At all costs, she wants a son. Eli thinks she's drunk out of her mind, as he witnesses the ordeal of her intercession. She's given over to grief and longing. I have only rarely felt that degree of sorrow. Once, at a Messianic Jewish conference in Northern Virginia, I began to imagine my relatives sinking into an inescapable hell. I could not stop weeping profusely. I was experiencing their separation from the goodness and mercy of God. It was awful and did not end quickly. For her sincere tears, Hannah receives the Lord's promise of childbirth and bears Samuel, the prophet.

Yeshua's Tears

Yeshua wept over Jerusalem. He couldn't look upon the city without envisioning its future destruction. His overwhelming desire was for the salvation of Israel. He is the archetype of the priesthood (see the Book of Hebrews), taking up a position between us on one side, in our futile state of fully deserved judgment—and God, on the other side, with His blameless, guilt-free adoption.

Although Yeshua came to the *"lost sheep of the House of Israel,"* His crucifixion meant redemption for the entire world. It was as if He "gave birth" to a new hope, a new reality for all human beings through His flesh. It's no accident that His suffering is termed the "passion." He allowed Himself to be pierced and ripped open for the sake of our excruciating need for atonement. This is comparable to a woman who endures the agony of labor pains in order to bring forth a new human being. It was His intercessory, priestly act on behalf of all mankind. He calls us to be "His body" in this world at this time, that He may intercede through us—bringing both Jews and Gentiles to their rebirth.

Shared priesthood is what the Lord showed me when I wept with a German prince over the lost condition of our nations. This privileged position, before the mercy seat of God, is the place He's calling us to occupy together. In kneeling as one, before the throne of Grace, coming before His presence as reunited Jewish and Gentile servants of the Living God—we will find the intervening power of God to redeem Israel. It is a humbling and unseen location, this place of weeping for Israel's lost sheep.

In the next chapter I parallel the resurrection of a man already buried, with the plight of Israel. I am convinced that the story of Lazarus provides a persuasive image of our current influential position at the tomb, the very site of Israel's resurrection.

Chapter Seven

Lazarus, Come Forth!

*Christians and Messianic Jews Prophesying to the Bones,
Call Israel Back to Life*

Then Solomon stood before the altar of the Lord in the presence of all the assembly of Israel and spread out his hands toward heaven; and he said "Lord God of Israel, there is no God in heaven above or on earth below like you, who keep your covenant and mercy with your servants who walk before you with all their hearts…When your people…have sinned against you and when they turn back to you and confess your name and pray and make supplication to you in this temple, then hear in heaven and forgive the sin of your people Israel, and bring them back to the land which you gave to their fathers.
1 Kings 8:22-23, 33-34

"Son of man, can these bones live?" So I answered, "O, Lord God, you know." Again He said to me, "Prophesy to these bones, and say to them, 'O dry bones, hear the word of the Lord! Thus says the Lord God to these bones: "Surely I will cause breath to enter into you and you shall live…Then you shall know that I am the Lord." ' " Ezekiel 37:3-6

Behold, O my people, I will open up your graves and cause you to come up from your graves, and bring you into the land of Israel...I will put my Spirit in you, and you shall live. Ezekiel 37:12, 14

A member of the congregation I served in the 1980s was stricken with the recurrence of a brain tumor. Several of us began to earnestly fast and pray, burdened that this vibrant young thirty-something businessman with a wife and two daughters not go to heaven prematurely. Pray and fast as we might, Michael's condition worsened steadily until he was confined to his bed at home, with every indication that he would soon die. A small group of us gathered one evening, knowing that our assignment was to stand with his wife until the very end, and if possible, to see him healed, even on his deathbed.

As the minutes dragged by, Michael's breathing became slower and weaker. Amidst the quiet prayers and praise, we listened and watched, feeling helpless to reverse death's claim. Then he stopped breathing. Gradually his skin paled, turning gray. The room filled up with impotent grief, as if a curling fog rose from the floor to engulf us. I kept looking at the man's face and thinking, "This shouldn't be happening!" Then, to quote an overused phrase, the thought came: "What would Yeshua do?" That question took my mind to the response of both Elijah (1 Kings 18:21) and Elisha (2 Kings 4:34) in similar situations. Both prophets lay on top of dead people in order to restore their life. The more I wrestled with that image the more I felt compelled to do it. I had no desire to indulge in presumptuous fanaticism, but I was determined to obey and wanted with all my heart for my friend to return to life. So, I summoned up my nerve and lay right on top of his fresh corpse. I put my mouth on his and pushed my breath into his mouth. Again and again, and again. It was useless. He was dead and I was not raising him. Only God can raise the dead, and it was evidently not His intention that night to do it through me.

When contemplating resurrection, we must look to what many consider the central prayer of the Jewish Prayer Book, *The Amidah*. This ancient prayer appeals to God based on His timeless attributes. Noticeably, the category most mentioned is the fact that it is God who raises the dead. He is described that way no less than six times in the opening paragraphs. Clearly our sages selected this as a capacity uniquely identifying the God of Israel. I agree with them and am indelibly sobered by the challenge of raising a dead man, since merely wanting to with all my heart was not enough to see that wonder take place.

Israel's Resurrection

Israel is an entire nation raised from the dead! The vision God gave Ezekiel in his 37th chapter is now a fact, approximately 2600 years after the prophet's encounter with the valley of dry bones. God asks Ezekiel a key question and then proceeds to give the answer.

And He said to me, "Son of man, can these bones live?" ...Thus says the Lord God to these bones: "Surely I will cause breath to enter into you and you shall live..." Ezekiel 37:3, 5

One facet that catches my attention is that God instructs the prophet to *"Prophesy to these bones and say to them '...you shall live...'"* There seems to be a required element of participation on the part of Ezekiel that God builds into the process. He must use his human voice and declare to the bones that which the Lord, who raises the dead, decrees. What does this have to do with us?

As a prophetic generation, I am convinced that it is our God-given assignment to do just what Ezekiel did. Yet this work is not for Messianic Jews to do alone. To illustrate how I see our joint participation in an Ezekiel-like prophetic role, I turn to a profound event in the New Covenant book of John. This story contains both of these elements, the

Resurrection of Israel and the Shared Priesthood of Jewish and Gentile believers, in bringing about that Resurrection. It is the story of Lazarus, the man whom Yeshua raised from the grave, told in John 11.

Lazarus represents Israel. Why do I conclude that so rapidly? The text gives us numerous clues.

1. **Lazarus had been dead a long time.** <u>Likewise, the nation of Israel was long in the grave.</u>

So, when Yeshua came, He found that he had already been in the tomb four days. John 11:17

2. **Lazarus' sisters are mourning bitterly** (11:19, 31). <u>The Jewish people as a whole are still mourning.</u>

This is the human backdrop of Israel as a nation. We have been in mourning, not for four days, but for century upon century. Look at our recent and ancient history. It includes Jihadist terrorism, the Holocaust (1935-1945), the Pogroms (racist massacres centered in Ukraine in the 1880's), the Inquisition (1480-1834; thousands of Jews were burned at the stake by the Catholic Church, some of them true believers in Yeshua who, like us, maintained their Torah-rooted practices), the Crusades (1095-1291), the destruction of both Temples (587 BCE and 70 CE) and outright expulsion from numerous countries.

3. **There is an atmosphere of grief and lost hope surrounding Martha and Miriam.** <u>This is exactly the condition of Israel following centuries of persecution, and especially in the aftermath of the Holocaust.</u>

We can see this same emotion prophetically in Naomi, the grieving mother in the Book of Ruth.

...it grieves me very much for your sakes that the hand of the Lord has gone out against me! Ruth 1:13

Do not call me Naomi [pleasant]*; call me Mara* [bitter]*, for the Almighty has dealt very bitterly with me. I went out full* [into the Diaspora] *and the Lord has brought me home again empty.* Ruth 1:20-21

In the case of Lazurus' sister, Miriam (whose name comes from the same root as *Mara*), the Jews accompanied her, as she wept with bitter disappointment that Yeshua had not been present (11:33).

4. Lazarus' family feels abandoned. Zion expresses this feeling too.

"If only you'd been there" (v.21) was the frustrated response. This is paralleled by the forlorn summary in Isaiah 49:14:

But Zion said 'The Lord has forsaken me, and my Lord has forgotten me.'

5. Yeshua "holds the key" to unlock Lazarus' grave. He still holds the key to unlock Israel's grave.

Miriam knew that Yeshua had resurrection power and fell at His feet in worship (11:32). She proclaimed, *"I believe you are the Messiah, the Son of God"* (John 11:27). This brings to mind the powerful phrase from the apocalyptic 2nd Psalm *"Kiss the Son..."* (Psalm 2:12). Of course, this is the authority that brings Israel to life from the dead, Yeshua's Kingship as the Greater Son of David.

The key of the house of David I will lay on His shoulder; so He shall

open, and no one shall shut; and He shall shut and no one shall open.
Isaiah 22:22

6. Yeshua weeps (11:35). <u>We are to be weeping priests.</u>

In the last chapter I wrote about Weeping Priests (Joel 2; Psalm 126; Jeremiah 9; and Hebrews 9-10 about the high priest). It is through our shared priesthood that we see the POWER of JEW and GENTILE interceding together. The prophet Joel highlights these priestly tears in Joel 2:17 and the Psalmist in Psalm 126:5-6. This is what happened to me with Prince Albrecht on Holocaust Remembrance Day (see Chapter 6: Shared Priesthood).

The key to God answering this resurrection prayer is intercessory weeping. That's why Yeshua wept. It wasn't so much that He was sad that Lazarus, His friend, died. I believe Yeshua was tuning into the way Lazarus represented the deadness of Israel and earnestly wanted His people to come to life. Our tears bring us together, with melted hearts, focused on the Salvation of Israel as the priority of God. We come to one table—the table of the Lord, the table of the New Covenant. Now we exercise our covenant entrance into the Holy of Holies, before the MERCY SEAT, to see Israel saved!

The Lord also wept in Luke 19. Yeshua stood overlooking Jerusalem, weighed down by the imminent exile and expelled state of the nation. Then, while driving out those who were buying and selling in the Temple precinct, He emphasized that the house of God is a house of prayer. So, for us, restoring God's house as a house of prayer is a key to Yeshua's return. How touching are the words of Isaiah in bringing Jew and Gentile together as agents of prayer-activated resurrection!

Also the sons of the foreigner [believing Gentiles] *who join themselves to the Lord, to serve Him and to love the name of the Lord, to be His servants—everyone who keeps from defiling the Sabbath, and holds fast my covenant—even them I will bring to my holy mountain, and make them joyful in my house of prayer...for my house shall be called a house of prayer for all nations.* Isaiah 56:6-7

7. **He says** *"Take away the stone"* (11:39)! <u>There are longstanding "stones" in Israel's path back to God.</u>

Let's put this in today's national terms. Removing the stone that covers our people's tomb is nothing less than taking away the stumbling blocks of anti-Semitism and replacement theology that have walled Jewish people away from their Messiah for nearly 2,000 years. As usual, Isaiah saw this coming.

The voice of one crying in the wilderness: "Prepare the way of the Lord; make straight in the desert a highway for our God...The crooked places shall be made straight and the rough places smooth; The glory of the Lord shall be revealed..." Isaiah 40:3-5a

Go through, go through the gates! Prepare the way for the people; Build up, build up the highway! Take out the stones, lift up a banner for the peoples! Isaiah 62:10

Yeshua removed the stone that sealed the tomb. But, Lazarus still had to walk out.

8. *"If you believe, you will see the glory of God"* (11:40). <u>If, in our generation we believe, we will see the glory of God.</u>

Isaiah 60 begins with an exhortation to Israel:

Arise, shine; for your light has come! And the glory of the Lord is risen upon you. Isaiah 60:1

All of Isaiah's Chapter 60 is about the glory of God. The word "glory" and its cognitives appear often in the prophets, occurring some 70 times in Isaiah alone. This unique revelation, to which I will devote all of the next chapter, speaks of the Jewish nation and Gentile nations in the latter days. Immediately after the prophet's declaration of the coming glory upon Israel, he includes the Gentiles who are drawn to the light that will shine upon her (60:3). There is a pre-planned interplay between Israel's resurrection and the faith involvement of the nations.

9. **Yeshua interceded before the Father at Lazarus' tomb** (11:41-42). <u>In a way, it was Israel's tomb.</u>

Yeshua, our High Priest interceded! This is the ONLY tomb where He interceded for resurrection. I am convinced that this is a picture of Yeshua's intercession for our Revival as a Nation. This is where we are prophetically, at this very moment. We are standing, as Yeshua's body on earth, in front of Lazarus'/Israel's tomb. Yeshua's assignment at the tomb was to take a stand as an intercessor who knew God's will and design. This is our assignment as well. God's will was to bring Lazarus out of his grave! The design He announced through His prophets, especially through Ezekiel, is to bring His nation of dry bones to life. We are centrally involved. We must take up our place at the door of Israel's tomb, pray together, and exercise faith for the resurrection.

10. **Yeshua stood, facing Lazarus' tomb.** <u>We, together, as His disciples, stand—facing Israel.</u>

Standing there, staring death in the face, Yeshua cried out with a loud voice. *"Lazarus, Come Forth"* (11:43)! These words energize me. I try to imagine that moment. There is electricity in the air. The Son of God is rebuking death and bringing a corpse back to life. We can compare Isaiah 51-52 where God calls upon Zion to awake, as if the nation is in death's slumber. Then he shifts into rapturous verses that describe the beauty of one who brings this good news of salvation.

How beautiful upon the mountains are the feet of him who brings good news, who proclaims peace, who brings glad tidings of good things, who proclaims salvation [yeshuah], who says to Zion, "Your God reigns!"... Break forth into joy, sing together, you waste places of Jerusalem!
Isaiah 52:7,9a

This is exactly what Lazarus does after being raised. He proclaims Salvation/Yeshua to his generation. Ironically, the chief priests and Pharisees plotted against Lazarus, and even more against Yeshua, from that day on.

11. *"Loose him and let him go"* (11:44). <u>Today, Israel is still struggling to get free.</u>

This was deliverance from death...unto life! It was a hint of what Ezekiel 37 will look like. There is a two-step process. First, we rise physically, with bones coming together, being clothed by sinews, flesh and skin (Ezekiel 37:7). But as a second phase, breath/spirit/wind (all three are the same word in biblical Hebrew-*ruach*) must enter the in-animate bodies. As I view Israel today, we have arisen, physically. We are alive again as a people, having a developed government, economy, military, media and education. But spiritually we have not yet come to life by God's Spirit. As a nation, we can only be made alive by the Spirit of the Living God—the same Spirit who raised Yeshua from the dead (Romans 8:11). Thousands of Israeli citizens are Messianic Jews, but 99.75 percent are not.

We are as Lazarus. I feel it, here in Israel. Our grave clothes must be removed. Years ago I was in Sao Paolo, Brazil. An odd "leading" came upon me. After delivering the evening's message, I felt that I was supposed to lie on the floor and be raised up by the hands of my brothers and sisters. The leadership confirmed it and I joined the congregation at the front of the sanctuary. I lay down, totally relaxed and tried to transform my thoughts to those of a man surrendered to death. Soon, I felt many hands and arms under me, lifting me up. It was such an amazing sensation. I felt entirely supported, not in need of anything and giddy with joy. As the people carried me around that room, singing and praising God, it was really as if I experienced His victory over death. By no accident, these were dedicated Gentile believers, holding me, a Messianic Jew, aloft, and proclaiming God's life from the dead.

> *Then He said to me, "Son of man, these bones are the whole house of Israel. They indeed say, 'Our bones are dry, our hope is lost, and we ourselves are cut off.' Therefore prophesy and say to them, 'Thus says the Lord God: "Behold, O my people I will open your graves and cause you to come up from your graves and bring you into the land of Israel. Then you shall know that I am the Lord, when I have opened your graves...I will put my Spirit in you, and you shall live, and I will place you in your own land...," says the Lord.' "* Ezekiel 37:11-14

Just as Lazarus had to have his grave clothes removed, we need to undergo repentance and revival. We are here. We are raised. But sometimes we stand immobilized. It's time to be mobilized. Yeshua said to those standing by: *"Loose him, and let him go."* We still need the help of the brothers and sisters viewing this whole phenomenon to get free, to be unbound.

12. *"Then many of the Jews...believed in Him"* (11:45). <u>We long for this to happen—soon!</u>

Lazarus must be fully raised (the body of Jews in Israel who follow Yeshua). What is the importance of the resurrection miracle? The

Apostle tells us in 1 Corinthians 1:22 that the Jews seek a sign. There is no greater sign than resurrection. The supernatural must be restored. This is why many Jewish people who lived in Israel in the first century believed in Him. Soon after Lazarus' resurrection from the dead:

...a great multitude that had come to the feast...took branches of palm trees and went out to meet Him, and cried out: "Hosanna!" John 12:12-13

The step that follows is to crown Yeshua as Israel's King. *"Baruch haBa baShem Adonai! Blessed is He who comes in the name of the Lord"* (Psalm 118:26; Matthew 23:39).

To summarize, here is the sequence that took place with Lazarus. The Lord is now calling us to participate in that same sequence. Priesthood brings Resurrection. First, Yeshua brings ISRAEL to life—true revival comes to the Messianic community in the land. This resurrection then attracts the attention of non-believers and they believe. Removing grave-cloths indicates a liberated community ready to proclaim Yeshua, a community that displays and draws the power of God as foretold by the prophets Ezekiel and Joel.

Weeping in intercession together, brings the resurrection of the long-dormant community of Messiah. Will we choose to live with courage and to follow Yeshua in His way?

You are reading this book because God is seeking to bring us into a strategic partnership—a relationship authored by the Most High. He is taking us into additional chapters of the Book. They are chapters He is inviting us to experience side by side. We are standing at the tomb of Lazarus. We are being called to make history together!

Here are the opportunities in each of your nations.

1. **REPRESENT** what God is doing in Israel through our work, Tents of Mercy, and other ministries.

2. **SHARE** the resurrection of Messianic Jews with fellow believers in your country through website, newsletter, prayer bulletin, and bringing tours to Israel.

3. **DEVELOP** your Israeli relationships with teams right here...to see this revival together.

King Solomon lifted up his hands and called on the name of the Lord on behalf of all Israel. It was a key moment of spiritual renewal made possible by the willing participation of the Gentiles who labored to build the Temple. We are again at such a time that calls for spiritual renewal in Israel. May our shared priesthood move the heart of God to send revival to this land.

Chapter Eight

Isaiah's Incredible Key

Five Essential Pillars of Gentile Participation in Israel's Redemption

And the king commanded them to quarry large stones, costly stones, and hewn stones, to lay the foundation of the temple. So, Solomon's builders and Hiram's builders and the Gebalites quarried them; and they prepared timber and stones to build the temple. 1 Kings 5:17-18

They came from North Carolina and Texas, Tennessee and Georgia, with names like Bill and Bob, Ray and Steve. They were electricians and carpenters, sheet-rockers and plumbers. They came with joy and love and prayer; and they brought their skills and their tools. In several waves they came, to help us build our facility near the Haifa Bay, in Kiryat Yam, Israel, as I recounted in Chapter One. It was a new spec building right next to the train tracks, in a "hidden" industrial area that almost nobody knew how to get to. Our friends from the nations changed it from an empty shell of concrete and cement block into a sanctuary, offices, classrooms, a kitchen, a distribution center, and a fellowship hall. Dedicated, good-natured guys came from America to create a congregational worship center, humanitarian aid center, and a place for the re-emerging Messianic community of Israel to manifest itself.

All of us who were there remember what it was like when we took huge steps forward in fashioning our facility in 1998, less than a year after we were fire bombed, and again in 2000, because we'd already outgrown the first sanctuary in our new building. The work of those teams, was a permanent and huge gift to the Tents of Mercy community. They created walls, laid tile floor, installed bathrooms, built cabinets and shelves and ran electric wires for sound and lighting.

So, when I read the following verse in Isaiah 60 I cannot help but apply it directly to the experience of receiving "sons of foreigners" who literally rebuilt our walls.

The sons of foreigners shall build up your walls, and their kings shall minister to you. Isaiah 60:10

But in order to explore the full and inclusive promises made in this chapter we need to go back to the first verses.

Arise, shine; for your light has come! And the glory of the Lord is risen upon you. For behold, the darkness shall cover the earth, and deep darkness the people; But the Lord will arise over you and His glory will be seen upon you. The Gentiles shall come to your light, and kings to the brightness of your rising. Isaiah 60:1-3

As with the rest of the biblical prophets, Isaiah's message was one of rebuke for sin, warning of coming judgment and exile, and the promise of a glorious future. These "seers" saw Israel restored to the land and revived as a people truly worshiping the Living God, purified from sin by the Lord of Hosts—our Redeemer. By the time we read Chapter 60, Isaiah has spoken of God's comfort to Israel (Chapter 40), God's Servant, who will establish justice in the earth, bear our sins, and make God known among the nations (Chapters 42, 43 and 53), and of God's Salvation bringing restoration to Israel and light to the Gentiles (Chapters 46, 49).

There is a crescendo in the Lord's voice declaring His divine, eternal intention to regather His people Israel. He is determined to bring us back to the portion of the earth He so often promised as our covenant home. This rhapsodic cascade of statements describing the return, repentance and revival of the Jewish people in Eretz Yisrael was immortalized by the melodies of George Frederick Handel. Handel's Messiah celebrates the coming of Yeshua the Messiah primarily through the words of Isaiah's prophecies. His oratorio anticipates not only the dramatic appearance of the Messiah as ultimate King over all the earth, but also the renewal of God's grace toward Yeshua's natural family, the Jewish people. The beginning of the entire, stirring composition is " 'Comfort, yes, comfort My people!' says your God" (Isaiah 40:1). These words declare the unchanging heart of God toward Israel and they set the stage for Isaiah's later description of the exiles' historic restoration as a nation in their own land.

At the outset of Isaiah 60 the Lord proclaims that His light will eventually shine again on Israel. Not only will Israel enter a new season of glory, but this will happen during a dark time in the future. Could the prophet have foreseen the darkness of the Holocaust and the miraculous rising up of Israel out of its ashes? From that exact reference in his next chapter, it would certainly seem so.

He has sent me to heal the brokenhearted, to proclaim liberty to the captives, And the opening of prison to those who are bound, to proclaim the acceptable year of the Lord...To comfort all who mourn, to console those who mourn in Zion, To give them beauty for ashes, the oil of joy for mourning, the garment of praise for the spirit of heaviness...
Isaiah 61:1-3

One ingredient in this rousing chapter sets it apart from nearly the entire body of prophetic scripture. It contains five full elements of Gentile participation in the phenomenon of Israel's restoration. When

Isaiah says *"Gentiles will come to your light"* he is opening a virtually un-explored area. It's an area touched on by Ezekiel in picturing the return of the exiles, but not described: *"...and the nations will know that you are the Lord"* (Ezekiel 36:23). Zechariah is among those who foresee the nations of the world joining in the celebration of the King's return to everlasting rule over all the earth (Zechariah 14:9). But this is much more. Isaiah gives detail and substance, providing a God-given task list for the Gentiles who are drawn to the light that will shine on Israel. The timing is precise! This phenomenon occurs as the stage of history prepares to receive the conquering Savior King, Yeshua HaMashiach.

For the Gentiles who *"come to the light,"* this is no mere spectator's role. God wants us to know the substantial place to which He is calling His followers among the nations. It is nothing less than midwifery, the job of the birthing coach and exhorter who enables the mother to bring forth her child. Here are the five facets I see in Isaiah 60.

1. ALIYAH (returning from the Diaspora to Israel)

He says *"...your sons shall come from afar, and your daughters shall be nursed at your side"* (60:4). This image is repeated in verses 8 and 9.

Who are these who fly like a cloud, and like doves to their roosts? Surely the coastlands shall wait for me; and the ships of Tarshish will come first, To bring your sons from afar, their silver and their gold with them, To the name of the Lord your God, and to the Holy One of Israel, because He has glorified you. Isaiah 60:8-9

What comes to mind are the airplanes and ships *(these who fly...the ships of Tarshish)* that are the very modes of transporta-tion already used to bring millions of Jewish people back to our ancient homeland. I flew in one of those "doves," immigrating to Israel with my wife and children from the *"coastlands"* of America in 1992. Some

Christian ministries with a heart to bring Jews to the shores of Israel, especially from the former Soviet Union—*"the land of the north"*—have literally chartered planes and ships. Names like Operation Jabotinsky, Operation Exodus, and the Ebenezer Fund made history by providing passage back to the Promised Land for those exiled from Israel nearly 2,000 years. Isaiah saw these Gentiles and their vessels of mercy.

2. RESOURCES

There will be an overflow of financial and material resources pouring in to Israel from Gentile friends.

And your heart shall swell with joy; because the abundance of the sea shall be turned to you, The wealth of the Gentiles shall come to you…they shall bring gold and incense, And they shall proclaim the praises of the Lord… Isaiah 60:5-6

Therefore your gates shall be open continually; they shall not be shut day or night, That men may bring to you the wealth of the Gentiles and their kings in procession. For the nation and kingdom which will not serve you shall perish, and those nations shall be utterly ruined. Isaiah 60:11-12

The multiplication of Gentile investments in Israel on every level has been astounding. In our twenty years in the land, we have seen an increase of church groups and Christians from literally every continent, eager to pour finances and aid into the land and the people of Israel. As Messianic Jews, we see this partnership as a natural outgrowth of our shared covenant in Yeshua. The Apostle Paul exhorted the Gentile believers in his letter to the Romans, saying *"…if the Gentiles have been partakers of their spiritual things, their duty is also to minister to them in material things"* (Romans 15:27).

3. INTERCESSION

When Isaiah says, *"Sons of foreigners will build up your walls"* (Isaiah 60:10), this can be applied literally, as I did in opening this chapter. Many ministries from the nations have done similar work and are continuing to do so. As an example, the work of the "Joshua Fund", launched by best-selling author, Joel Rosenberg, has crisscrossed Israel and the Middle East, sowing the resources donated by devoted Christians. The investment in "building up the walls" is huge. And this is only one of many Christian ministries placing tools in the hands of Israel's resurgent believing community.

But this prophecy can also be applied spiritually. Here's what I mean. Two chapters later, God declares:

I have set watchmen on your walls, O Jerusalem; They shall never hold their peace day or night. You who make mention of the Lord, do not keep silent, and give Him no rest till He establishes and till He makes Jerusalem a praise in the earth. Isaiah 62:6-7

These verses are widely understood to describe the spiritual work of intercessory prayer that must come before the Lord, until He restores Israel to her full glory as a resurrected people, worshiping Him and embracing their King, Yeshua. That's the way I interpret this passage. Therefore, when the same prophet refers to *"walls"* a few pages earlier, I am compelled to apply this definition to the ones who rebuild those walls. So, the *"sons of foreigners"* who are doing the wall building are none other than our Gentile brothers and sisters *"who make mention of the Lord"* (62:6). This is exciting! It means that God anticipated the urgent need for the nations to pray strong prayers of intercession on behalf of Israel, at the end of the age. In utter and astonishing fulfillment of this prophetic portrait, there are thousands of focused prayer groups across the globe, devoting themselves to being *"watchmen on the walls,"* imploring the

Ruler of the Universe to restore Jerusalem as His kingdom headquarters.

4. TURNING from Anti-Semitism

Next, is the sobering statement in verse fourteen:

Also the sons of those who afflicted you shall come bowing to you, and all those who despised you shall fall prostrate at the soles of your feet; And they shall call you the City of the Lord, Zion of the Holy One of Israel. Isaiah 60:14

The first time I ever stepped foot in Germany was difficult. There were emotional reminders of our past *"affliction"* as a people *"despised"* in that nation. But God caught me by surprise as I took part in a gathering of German and Israeli leaders, all followers of Yeshua. We were visiting the Wannsee Mansion, outside Berlin. This stately building now houses a Holocaust museum, but in 1943 it was the site where Hitler's high command devised "The Final Solution." Our group met upstairs, where the despicable discussion took place—plotting the absolute eradication of the Jewish people. Sobered, turning to the Lord, we all began to worship softly in brokenness. Soon, every heart turned its attention to the mercy of God. Surrounded by the memory of such hatred and slaughter, what else could we do?

Slowly, our German counterparts slipped down to the floor, burying their faces in the carpet, right next to our feet. Just as the prophet envisioned, those of the very generation whose fathers had sent us to mass death in the ovens were now prostrating themselves before us! Not content to have people bowing before us, and being moved by the same Spirit, we responded in kind, assuming a prone position beside them. Soon, the entire floor was covered with Germans and Jews, worshiping Yeshua and weeping in intercession for each other's people. It was the most literal fulfillment of Isaiah 60:14 I could have imagined.

5. NURTURE

Finally, comes the enigmatic verse 16. A veritable biological impossibility, nonetheless the prophet declares that we will *"drink the milk of the Gentiles, and milk the breast of kings."* Hmmm? What is he talking about? The image that came to me immediately was from 1 Peter 2:2: *"...as newborn babes desire the pure milk of the word..."* Of course, what other milk could I receive from Gentiles, but that of the Word? Then I remembered the dedicated, sincere, wise Bible teachers I had in the 1970s. They were Gentile kings (in the spiritual sense); and they certainly invited me to drink of their knowledge—to be fed by the rich, creamy milk of the Spirit that nourished me in that foundational time.

Even now, important Bible teaching and coaching come from our Gentile brothers. It's true that in the past 30 years, my Messianic Jewish brothers and sisters have contributed many books, and historic breakthroughs in understanding God's purposes. And long before our generation, Jewish teachers have provided spiritual insights for millennia. Yet the majority of His Spirit birthed instruction is still being received from non-Jewish sources. The prophet finishes verse 16 with this:

You shall know that I, the Lord, am your Savior and your Redeemer, the Mighty One of Jacob.

He is linking the knowledge of God—His saving grace and the end-time revelation of His Majesty the King—to the joint venture of the Jewish and Gentile disciples of Yeshua at the end of the age. Wow!

The boulders and timber that Solomon and Hiram used were not able to bear the weight of God's glory to the degree that we can, as Jewish and Gentile living stones, built together to be one house.

Chapter Nine

Return of the Lost Son

An Ancient Parable Predicts a Contemporary Phenomenon

But when he came to himself, he said..., "I will arise and go to my father, and will say to him, 'Father, I have sinned against heaven and before you, and I am no longer worthy to be called your son. Make me like one of your hired servants.'" Luke 15:17-19

In this chapter we will look into the significance of the lost son in Yeshua's parable. But first allow me to share the story of a different prodigal. I know what it is to be a lost son. I was one. Born into 1950s prosperity and assimilated into American culture, I grew up in Southern California during that region's boom era. It was as if the entire nation suddenly realized that the "Golden" State was the locale for movies, TV, surfing, and Disneyland. My mother was Jewish, my father the Gentile child of Bulgarian, orthodox Christian immigrants. My parents were both liberal humanists in philosophy, politics, and religion. Therefore, the only "church/synagogue" experience they could tolerate was Unitarian Universalism. We were neither Jewish nor Christian.

By my teen years, I thought I knew more about life than they did. *So, I left home.* Though we maintained good contact during those searching years, after graduating from high school I never lived at home again.

Once I grasped how painful and difficult life's challenges were, I realized that it is not so easy to turn the world around. Maybe I was on my way to a "prodigal son" awakening. Seemingly, the more I dedicated myself to ending war and intolerance, the more difficult those goals were to achieve. By the end of 1967 I was sitting in jail, convicted of "disturbing the peace" during an anti-war demonstration. I began to wonder. Was I really becoming a better person through all this? Or had my heart become harder as I attempted to change the system, opposing what I thought was wrong, but failing to provide any real alternative? At this point, I really felt distant from my conventional parents.

Next, I met my true love, Connie. Though we did not yet know the Lord and had grown up on opposite sides of the U.S.A., He somehow miraculously joined our lives together. It's too long a story to tell here, but there were many incidents of God's providence and grace. We got married in January of 1969 and immediately set out for the Land of Enchantment—New Mexico, to start our new communal life of farming and returning to nature. Several years into our lengthy experiment a very close friend was murdered by a stranger passing through. This felt like the end of our dream. The experiment had failed. We had not created utopia, rather we had lost a beloved brother. Now I had nowhere to turn. So, I turned upward to heaven and cried out to a God I had never met. I wasn't even sure He existed. "If you're up there, I'd like to know what happened to my friend, and why things are not working out the way we thought they would."

This desperate prayer was answered, in a totally unexpected way, by the arrival of some hip-looking guys from the "East Coast" who were just staying for the winter on the other side of the mountains. One evening, as they told us about the love of God, about Yeshua's miracle-working personality, and about His self-emptying sacrifice, I had a vision. I saw Him. I saw Yeshua on the cross while He was dying for me. It was so riveting, so revelatory that I was convinced then and now (more than forty years later) that this was the answer I'd been seeking. I knelt down with my buddy, Russell, another Jewish refugee from the city, and asked Jesus to forgive me for violating God's purity. I said, "Come into my heart. Please." He forgave me, cleansed me, and I began a new voyage that I could not possibly have imagined.

It was only through the transformation of my heart, inhabited by Yeshua upon salvation, that my relationship with my mom and dad really changed. I repented for causing them so much grief. I began praying for them. Our visits were always a special reunion, enriched by the companionship of my wife, Connie, and our four children, David, Hannah, Avi and Sigal. In time, while still a relatively young believer, I returned to my lost Jewish heritage, discovering the Hebraic roots of the New Covenant. Although my folks never openly embraced Yeshua, I know they greatly appreciated the changes they witnessed in me. They were able to see the lifelong stability of our family, rooted in covenant with God.

After a life of street protests, drug use, rock gigs, and country communes—I came "home." Even having a normal telephone number my parents could call was revolutionary. We rejoined the economy and society of the United States of America after nearly six years of seeking a primitive substitute in the mountains of northern New Mexico (January 1969-October 1974). We embraced these "compromises" with our ideal of an ecologically pure, organic existence, because we knew there were many other lost sons and daughters out there. Maybe we could help them get home.

My father and mother both died at the age of 94 in 2011. I loved them very much. Dad was strong, practical, and totally devoted to his family. Mom was a brilliant and creative woman. She was a teacher, a writer, and was hooked on travel. Making the long trips to Oregon to be with my sister and care for them together, during their final days, was one of the deepest experiences of my life. It was not easy. But God gave me His heart for my father and mother. That's just what happened to the Prodigal Son.

A Lost Son

In the Luke 15 story, one son takes his inheritance early, while his father still lives. Some commentators have pointed out that this was a real insult, a slap in the face, to his dad. Another word for it is *chutzpah*. The son launches out, hoping for adventure, fun, maybe even fame. One problem is, of course, that his finances run out well before he expects. Another major difficulty is that he burned his bridges behind him. His relationships back home are broken. He has become arrogant, selfish, and callously independent. He winds up among the hogs, in the pen with them, no less!

Doesn't the picture of the Prodigal leaving his father's house remind you of our people? Once I began to see this as a picture of the departure of the Jewish people from the household of God I couldn't shake it. I know that it violates the typical formula of "older son=the Jews; younger son=the Gentiles." But just put that aside for a moment, please. There's something here that God wants to point out. If we see the prodigal as "taking his inheritance" and scattering both his gifts and talents out in the "hinterland," away from home—might we see a metaphor of the Jewish people in Exile? Yes, we've been blessed in certain places, in certain eras, among the Gentiles. At the same time, through striving, suffering and dedication, we have maintained a vestige of our calling to be a people of covenant. But the bottom line is that until the founding of the modern state of Israel, with its "Law of Return," we've been wandering, and the blessing has been more residual than immediate.

In Yeshua's story, the lost son comes to himself. Verses 17-18 are the turning point. Prophetically, this parallels Deuteronomy 30:1-3, 5 and Hosea 3:4-5, which speak about Israel returning to the Lord after "*many days"* while still in the Diaspora:

> *Now it shall come to pass, when all these things have come upon you, the blessing and the curse which I have set before you, and you call them to mind among all the nations where the Lord your God drives you, and you return to the Lord your God and obey His voice, according to all that I command you today...that the Lord your God will bring you back from captivity, and have compassion on you, and gather you again from all the nations where the Lord your God scattered you...Then the Lord your God will bring you to the land which your fathers possessed, and you shall possess it. He will prosper you and multiply you more than your fathers.* Deuteronomy 30:1-3, 5

> *For the children of Israel shall abide many days without king or prince, without sacrifice or sacred pillar, without ephod or teraphim. Afterward the children of Israel shall return and seek the Lord their God and David their king. They shall fear the Lord and His goodness in the latter days.* Hosea 3:4-5

The disillusioned lad repents. *"Father, I have sinned against heaven and against you."* What happens next, poignantly reflects the merciful nature of God, so that we are touched deeply again and again, each time we read it. The father's incredible compassion demonstrates the heart of God for "wayward" Israel. The parallels are simply too powerful to bypass.

The Father's Forgiving Embrace

In the next scene we see the father running to his son and embracing him, not blaming or scolding him. This is a dad who has interceded, probably every day. It's a dad who has been longing for the restoration of his son, not his destruction.

Can a woman forget her nursing child?...Surely they may forget, yet I will not forget you. Isaiah 49:15

Can a virgin forget her ornaments or a bride her attire? Yet my people have forgotten me days without number. Jeremiah 2:32

...Come and let us join ourselves to the Lord in a perpetual covenant that will not be forgotten. Jeremiah 50:5

I will betroth you to Me forever... Hosea 2:19

Lord, forever? I hear Him saying "Yes, for all time Israel will be my beloved. Nothing will permanently separate us. You have come back, against all odds, as I always believed you would." His ultimate statement is *"My son was dead and is alive again"* (Luke 15:24). It is relevant here to recall that the *Amidah*, the central prayer in Judaism, declares several times that it is God who raises the dead (see Chapter 7: Lazarus, Come Forth!).

The story Yeshua told is not only about God's heart for sinners who repent. It is symbolic of the heart of Father God for His sheep, Israel, who have wandered for nearly twenty centuries among the nations. We have spent our "inheritance" trying to establish life outside the land of Israel. But it has been to no avail. We only have one home—Israel. This is where we belong. Help us return. Help us flourish here. Help us get back to our Father. We need help from our Gentile brethren, from the brother who stayed home.

Meanwhile, back at the ranch, the older brother is "ticked off," to say the least. He claims, "I have served you these many years (think of the history of "The Church"). You never gave me anything. Now this profligate, reprobate son of yours thinks he can just waltz in here and pick up where he left off. No way. I draw the line." If this doesn't smack of Replacement Theology, I don't know what does.[5] It is exactly what Paul was addressing in Romans 11:17-24 when he said essentially, "Don't boast. The same thing can happen to you." The resentful brother is boasting: "Now we (the Church) are Israel. The lost son lost his place. He rebelled. It's my inheritance now. Forget him. Even if he (Israel) is back, he can serve on my terms, and mine alone."

The father, beside himself with joy, responds to the self-righteous son; "You didn't lose anything because of his return. The kingdom is still yours. My house has many mansions. You're missing the point. Your brother (Israel) was dead and now he's alive. He was lost, but now he's found." This echoes Isaiah's joyful proclamation:

So the ransomed of the Lord shall return, and come to Zion with singing, with everlasting joy on their heads. They shall obtain joy and gladness; Sorrow and sighing shall flee away. Isaiah 51:11

I want to propose an alternate ending to this story. It carries the message of this book. I hear the heart of the Father appealing to the "stay at home" son, His Church, to celebrate with Him the miraculous return of the Jewish son. For Israel to come back to Yeshua is truly like the Lost Son coming home.

In this God-pleasing response, I see believers around the world coming to a "banquet" thrown by God Himself. They are praising the Father for the rebirth of Jewish men and women through the Gospel of Yeshua HaMashiach. I see a Joyful Brother in the place of the Resentful Brother pictured in Scripture. He is rejoicing with us. As Jeremiah 31:7 declares: *"Sing with gladness for Jacob, and shout among the chief of the nations; Proclaim, give praise, and say, 'O Lord save your people, the remnant of Israel.'"*

Chapter Ten

Is the Torah for Gentiles?

Seeking Answers for Honest, Urgent Questions

Since we have heard that some who went out from us have troubled you with words, unsettling your souls, saying, "You must be circumcised and keep the law"—to whom we gave no such commandment—it seemed good to us, being assembled with one accord, to send chosen men to you with our beloved Barnabas and Paul. Acts 15:24-25

We live in a day when the Spirit is inspiring many Christians to love Israel and to appreciate the Jewish roots of the New Covenant. This is a welcome revolution. After nearly 1,800 years of anti-Semitism in the name of Jesus Christ, the Jewish people are ready for the honor and affection now coming from portions of the Church. *Shofars* can be heard in church services. Israeli flags and banners proclaiming the Hebrew roots of New Covenant faith can be seen in the sanctuaries of Christian congregations. This is a major historic change! In the past forty years we have seen the rise of many ministries devoted to supporting Israel.

They are increasing overall awareness of the Gospel's Jewish roots and are helping Jewish people find their Messiah without having to become Gentiles.

With such a wave of visionary enthusiasm, it is understandable that the Jewish way of life now looks attractive to Gentile believers with a heart for Israel. How can we know where the balance is? What is required? What is allowed? Must everyone live according to Torah, both Jew and Gentile? If not, how can the Gentile believer express solidarity with the Jewish believer?

First, the clear teaching both of the New Covenant and of the Hebrew Scriptures is that keeping the Law of Moses does not bring salvation. Salvation is by grace through faith for all who believe, both Jew and Gentile (Genesis 15:6; Habakkuk 2:4; Ephesians 2:8; Romans 1:16; Galatians 2:16). Therefore, an individual cannot be "more saved" or "more spiritual" by embracing the requirements of Torah. If so, the utter value of the blood of Messiah would be diminished.

Filled with strong feelings, convictions and offenses, we do well to ask a few clarifying questions. It would be presumptuous to even attempt answering all the questions being asked on this subject. But here are a few of the main ones, along with some basic answers. I readily admit that the questions and theological orientations raised in this chapter are not the easiest to address. They require balance and humility. Let's seek to work through them together.

1. What is the purpose of Torah?
2. How did the Apostles understand the Acts 15 decision?
3. What was the outworking of that decision in the first century—on site?
4. Doesn't all this render the Gentile believer a "second class citizen" in the kingdom?
5. What about the Two-Covenant theory?
6. Is there any truth to what the Ephraimites are teaching?

7. Can we say that there is "One Law" for Israel and the same law for the Church?

1. What is the purpose of Torah?

The Law of Moshe was given to Israel as a covenant, connected to our dwelling in the land as the descendants of Abraham, Isaac and Jacob. Living by the Torah is to be a testimony to the faithfulness of God and the vehicle to bring His Messiah into the world—through the nation of Israel.

We must understand the Scriptures in their original context. "Becoming a Jew" in the ears of the first century Apostles meant conforming to Torah, including circumcision—the sign of Torah observance. Any male convert to Judaism had to be circumcised. This command is an integral (and intimate) part of Torah. *Then He gave him the covenant of circumcision* (Acts 7:8). Nowhere in Torah is circumcision separated from the keeping of the law or keeping of the law separated from circumcision.

There are some Gentile enthusiasts for the Torah who strongly advocate that other non-Jewish followers of Jesus "keep the Torah." And yet they draw the line short of circumcision. Why? Is this according to the Torah itself? Is it the way our first century spiritual ancestors understood becoming a literal part of Israel? This was not their understanding.

It will help to look at Exodus 12:43-49. There the meaning is clear. If you join yourselves to us through the Torah, God requires you to remove your foreskin. The clear context is the "stranger" (*ger*) living among us, in the land. It relates to those who choose to enter the physical nation of Israel. So, in Exodus 12, the stranger receives the command to be circumcised, in order to celebrate Passover:

And when a stranger dwells with you and wants to keep the

Passover to the Lord, let all his males be circumcised, and then let him come near and keep it, and he shall be as a native of the land. For no uncircumcised person shall eat it. One law shall be for the native-born and for the stranger who dwells among you. Exodus 12:48-49

One law for the native-born and for the stranger *"who dwells among you."* This relates to permanent physical residence amidst Israel and overtly includes the physical sign of circumcision as part and parcel of the deal.

The word *ger* (stranger), coming from the Hebrew verb *la'GUR* (to live, reside in a place), was used to designate a person who was not born an Israelite, but by virtue of living in the land became a part of the people. Its first appearance is in Genesis 15:13 where God tells Abraham *"Know certainly that your descendants will be strangers in a land that is not theirs."* This status requires a *ger* to eat unleavened bread during Passover (Exodus 12:19), but only after being circumcised (Exodus 12:48)! He was also to experience the same death penalty as a native-born murderer (Leviticus 24:16).

Paul is clear about circumcision (1 Corinthians 7:17-20). The whole context of that discussion is *"remaining as you were."* It is preceded by a discussion about the unmarried, widows, those married to non-believers, etc. Why did he keep saying that neither circumcision nor uncircumcision, neither Jew nor Greek, were important? It was because guys were running around saying "You gotta be circumcised and keep Torah in order to follow Yeshua correctly." And he was standing against that.

2. How did the Apostles understand the Acts 15 decision?

The first Apostles already wrestled with this very question of Torah-keeping for Gentile believers. Some of the sect of the Pharisees who believed, rose up saying *"It is necessary to circumcise them, and to command them to keep the law of Moses"* (Acts 15:5). In response, Peter recounted the way the Spirit fell upon the household of Cornelius (Acts 10), without *"distinction."* In the Apostles' definitive letter, they wrote:

> *Since we have heard that some...have troubled you with words, unsettling your souls, saying, "You must be circumcised and keep the law"—to whom we gave no such commandment.* Acts 15:24

This sounds just like the controversy of today. And their answer could not be clearer.

> *For it seemed good to the Holy Spirit, and to us, to lay upon you no greater burden than these necessary things: that you abstain from things offered to idols, from blood, from things strangled, and from sexual immorality. If you keep yourselves from these you will do well.* Acts 15:28-29

3. What was the outworking of that decision in the first century— on the ground?

Five times in Acts 15, the statement is made that the Gentile believers are not required to keep the law (vv. 5, 10, 19, 24 and 28). Peter declared, "[God] *made no distinction between us and them, purifying their hearts by faith*" (Acts 15:9). Interestingly, the accusation leveled against Paul was not that he failed to lead the Gentiles to a Torah based lifestyle. On the contrary, he was falsely accused of teaching Messianic Jews to forsake the law. Later, Paul's companions in Jerusalem urged him to take a vow with them in order to settle the situation once and for all. They wanted to differentiate between Paul's Jewish way of following Yeshua and the way for the Gentile disciples. They persuaded him to prove that:

> *...you yourself also walk orderly and keep the law. But concerning the Gentiles who believe, we have written and decided that they should*

observe no such thing, except that they should keep themselves from things offered to idols, from blood, from things strangled and from sexual immorality. Acts 21:24-25

The onsite outworking of the Apostles' decision was that Jewish followers of Yeshua were to continue in their calling as those identifiably within Israel. And at the same time, Gentile followers of Yeshua were no longer to assume that they needed to convert to Judaism. Rather, their faith in Yeshua as Lord and Savior was sufficient to bring them into kingdom citizenship with those born Jewish.

4. Doesn't all this render the Gentile believer a "second-class citizen" in the kingdom?

So, if the Gentile believer in Jesus is not required to be circumcised and to keep Torah, is he allowed to? May he keep part but not all? Since the first century disciples of Yeshua celebrated the feasts of Israel (Leviticus 23) and understood their Messianic significance, His twenty-first century disciples of all nations are free to celebrate them too. In doing so, the Gentile believer affirms the eternal value of these prophetic festivals, and identifies himself as a friend of Israel. Through the feasts, through support for the nation of Israel, through intercession, through teaching and rejoicing in the Jewish roots of the New Covenant—through all these, solidarity is expressed with the Jewish people, without second-class status.

But is there a different origin to this question of "should Gentiles keep the Torah?" Could it be rooted more in the issue of personal value than in theological debate? In some subtle way has the Messianic movement sent a signal that God prefers Jews, making it better/superior to be Jewish? Should the Gentile believer, for instance, be jealous of the Jewish national calling? Some are even converting to Judaism, hoping to show their zeal.

I want to begin my answer by repenting on behalf of our movement, the modern Messianic Jewish movement. At times intentionally (God, forgive us!), and at other times unintentionally, we have implied that Gentiles were "not quite as important to God" as Jews. Oh, beloved, this is not the case. *"For God so loved the WORLD, that He gave His only begotten Son"* (John 3:16). Please forgive us, the Messianic Jews, for in any way communicating the lie that Gentiles are less important to God than we are. It is not true.

He loves the people of the nations NO LESS than the people of Israel. We have unique callings, just as we have unique anatomical features as male and female. It is this parallel that the Spirit wisely uses to help us comprehend our coexistence. The reason jealousy has no place between men and women or between Jew and Gentile is that God created us both with equal value.

5. What about the Two-Covenant Theory?

The two-covenant theory is popular among those who do not want to offend the Jewish community and are loathe to say that Yeshua is THE way to the God of Israel. Our first job is to remain liberated from interpreting the Bible according to what is convenient to us, or according to what makes it easier to relate to a given group of people. Of course, we are to avoid causing unnecessary offense. There have been many unnecessary offenses against the Jews during Christian history. Those offenses have been voluminously documented.

Yes, the Church has much of which to repent. Yes, it is time for believers to see the anti-Semitism of past generations and eschew it. And, yes, there is an historic awakening that is sweeping the world, bringing Jesus' people back to His own roots. Yet the New Covenant was specifically given first to Israel. Nothing could be clearer in Scripture than the fact that Yeshua came first for the Jewish people, to be their sin-bearer and King.

The two-covenant theory says that the Jewish people have a different covenant of salvation from the Gentiles. This flies straight in the face of the Jewish Scriptures. It is the Hebrew prophet Jeremiah who first enunciates the New Covenant, not a Gentile preacher:

> *Behold the days are coming, says the Lord, when I will make a new covenant with the house of Israel and with the house of Judah—not according to the covenant that I made with their fathers in the day that I took them by the hand to lead them out of the land of Egypt, my covenant which they broke, though I was a husband to them, says the Lord. But this is the covenant that I will make with the house of Israel after those days, says the Lord: I will put my law in their minds, and write it on their hearts, and I will be their God and they shall be my people.* Jeremiah 31:31-33

When we consider the "outrage" caused among the Jewish people by mentioning that Yeshua came to bring a new covenant to Israel, one would think this passage does not exist. But it does. It cannot be erased from the Hebrew Bible. Nowhere does God suggest that the basis of salvation is different for Israel than for the nations.

In fact, there are many places in both the Hebrew and the Greek Scriptures that make it clear that Yeshua came to bring God's salvation to Israel—first and foremost. *"Salvation is of the Jews"* (John 4:22) may be His most radical statement on the subject. The first chapter of Luke makes it clear that the Messiah is the expression of God's mercy to Israel in bringing salvation. First, Miriam magnifies the Lord concerning her expected Son, the Promised One. Then Zacharias, filled with the Spirit, prophesies about his son, John the Immerser.

> *He* [the Lord God] *has helped His servant Israel, in remembrance of His mercy, as He spoke to our fathers, to Abraham and to his seed forever.* Luke 1:54-55

And you, child…will go before the face of the Lord to prepare His ways, to give knowledge of salvation to His people [Israel] *by the remission of their sins through the tender mercy of our God.* Luke 1:76-78

Some offenses need to be removed. Some will have to remain. It is stated unequivocally that there is only one way to reach the Father. That is through His Son, Yeshua (John 14:6). But in our desire to make life less complicated for the Jewish people, who've suffered enough, let's not compromise the truth of the Word of God. We cannot expunge guilt from the Christian Church, which has committed horrid atrocities in the name of the Jewish Messiah, by removing the offense of the Gospel (see Romans 9:32, 33; Isaiah 8:14). He came FIRST and foremost for the Jews. *"I was not sent except to the lost sheep of the house of Israel"* (Matthew 15:24). If we pretend there is a different, saving covenant for the Jewish people, just because we're Jewish, then we remove the priority of introducing us to our own Messiah King! This would be tragic. Paul wrote:

I am not ashamed of the Gospel of Messiah, for it is the power of God to salvation for everyone who believes, for the Jew first and also for the Greek [Gentile]. Romans 1:16

6. Is there any truth to what the Ephraimites are teaching?

In the Ephraimite teaching much is made of the two sticks of Ezekiel in Chapter 37. Those who hold to this view are thereby called "Ephraimites." This theory was popularized by Batya Wootten in her book *Who is Israel?* (Key of David, St. Cloud, Florida, 1998). Adherents of this view believe that all, or nearly all, born-again Christians are, in fact, members of the Northern tribes of Israel who were "scattered" after the Assyrian Exile. Ephraimites support the keeping of Torah for Gentiles (aka Israel), with the exception of circumcision (see my discussion earlier in this chapter).

One of the most complete responses to this theology, available on-line, is Dr. Kay Silberling's paper, "The Ephraimite Error." It details the nature of the doctrine and gives an excellent refutation. Silber-ling states that, according to the "Two House" theory, "It is now incumbent upon these members of 'Ephraim'…to 'accept their birthright' and live as members of Israel."[6] In her research, Silberling points out the obvious regarding this serious error. Ephraimites so blur the distinction between Israel (the Jewish people) and the Gentiles (those not born of Jewish parents) that it borders on reverse Replacement Theology. Replacement Theology (supercessionism) says that the Church is Israel and that God's promises of a fulfilled relationship with Him now belong to the Church, since Israel broke covenant with God. The Two House theory also says the Church is Israel, but instead of affirming the Gentile identity of the church it transposes a Jewish identity on to the Church. Either way Israel looses its identity within the Gentile church and is thereby replaced.

The Ephraimites maintain that since there are so many truly believing disciples of Yeshua, the way to understand God's goal of ultimate union, is to call the genuine Christians "Israel" (i.e. Ephraim) and those who are natural Jews "Judah." Thus the two sticks in Ezekiel 37 are Christians and Messianic Jews.

As for you, son of man, take a stick for yourself and write on it: "For Judah and for the children of Israel, his companions." Then take another stick and write on it, "For Joseph, the stick of Ephraim, and for all the house of Israel, his companions." Then join them one to another for yourself into one stick, and they will become one in your hand. Ezekiel 37:16-17

Their goal is good and biblical. The unity of Messianic Jews and true Christians is no less than one of this book's primary messages. However, the abuse of Scripture, history and common sense is alarming and needs to be exposed. I entirely support the message of Ezekiel, that God will *"take the children of Israel from among the nations…and make them one nation in the land…"* (Ezekiel 37:21-22). But it will not help the cause of unity or the Jewish Roots of the New Covenant to confuse the true identity of the Jewish people and that of the Gentile nations.

In fact, the origin of this error is, in my view, the incorrect and unhealthy effort to gain identification with Israel via the twisting of Scripture. Why do all Christians need to be Israel? It would seem that there is a hidden agenda. If we say that all Christians are really Israel, but have not known it, then we are all one big family with no more need to deal with either the Jewish community (which surely is confused and put off by this claim) or the "division" between Jewish and Gentile believers. It is based on the false need for non-Jewish believers to feel that they are "just as good" as natural born Jews, on the basis of discovering their "true identity" as Israel. The whole teaching flows from a sense of inferiority that is neither biblical nor in any way God's intent.

This claim, besides being evidentially untrue, negates the message of the New Covenant and the work of Yeshua to (a) save Israel and (b) bring His Jewish and Gentile followers together.

7. Can we say that there is "One Law" for Israel and the same law for the Church?

The last position I will examine on the question of "Torah for the Gentiles" is the so-called "One Law" doctrine, taken from the verses that say *"One law and one custom shall be for you and for the stranger who dwells with you"* (Numbers 15:16).

In responding to this question, we will make liberal use of a paper published by my two dear friends, Daniel Juster and Russell Resnik, entitled "One Law Movements." Juster (a mentor and foundational influence on my life) and Resnik (life-time friend and "spiritual twin" from the New Mexico days) point out that a healthy starting point in evaluating this concept is to review the attitude of the historic church to the law of God. The authors emphasize that until the 19th century, most theologies, notably the influential work of John Calvin (16th century author of Reformed theology) had a positive view of God's law. The problem with this orientation is that Reformed theology saw the Church replacing Israel. Ironically, while validating the Torah as the basis of God's way of life for Christians, Calvin and others denied Israel's access to the permanent covenant with Abraham, Isaac and Jacob. Thus, many of Jesus' followers have seen the validity of God's moral law through the centuries, even as they rejected the chosen role of Israel.

A later, contrasting viewpoint was pioneered by J.N. Darby and popularized in the "Schofield Bible." Theirs is the Dispensational view that Christians are not to be concerned with the "law" since Jesus came to inaugurate a "dispensation of grace" whereby we are no longer "under the law" but freed from the law. Such freedom focuses on the Epistles of Paul, down-playing even the Torah orientation of Yeshua Himself. In the plus column, dispensationalists tend to embrace Israel as the fulfillment of God's promises to restore the nation to its original homeland. The downside is a negative view of the Torah as an expression of God's will with continued application.

So, why is there not "one law," the same one, for Israel and for the Church? The simple answer is that the Torah is addressed to a specific, physical group of people, the literal descendants of Abraham, Isaac and Jacob. Our nation, the Jewish people/Israel, has been preserved for some 4,000 years, which is itself an amazing feat within history. As discussed elsewhere, the Apostles examined this issue of Gentile adherence to the Torah at length, early in the history of Yeshua's followers. Their conclusion was recorded in Acts 15 in order to bring understanding and unity. This unity was not to be at the cost of blurring the Creator's distinction between Jew and Gentile. Rather, it was to free the Gentile believers from an obligation to live according to the full requirements of the Law of Moses, the Torah. This was not a put-down, or a marginalization. It was, for that time, a radical realization that Yeshua had created a new foundation for Jew and Gentile alike. That foundation was His sacrificial death and resurrection. Had the Apostles intended for Gentile disciples to apply the same Mosaic Law to themselves as the Jewish believers, they could have easily said so. But they made absolutely no mention of that term or of the "One Law" verses: Exodus 12:49, Leviticus 24:22 and Numbers 15:16.

Yes, there are many passages and principles that apply to all who love God and His ways. Yeshua and the writers of the New Covenant quote from the *Tanakh* as their exclusive source of written truth. Yet this validation does not equal "one law" for all believers. The context, as mentioned previously, is that of the *ger*, who lives physically within the borders of Israel and chooses to adopt all of the Torah, including circumcision. Galatians 5 warns Gentiles not to receive circumcision or they will be required to keep the whole Torah. "The clear implication is that without circumcision, Gentiles are not required to keep the whole Torah."[7]

New Covenant Texts and "Torah for the Gentiles"

W.D. Davies, a groundbreaking scholar in the field of the Jewish background of the New Testament, wrote the following conclusion from the Acts controversy over Gentiles and the Torah of Moshe. "One could be a Christian without being a Jew so the doors were open to the Gentiles."[8]

The implications of Davies's statement answer many if not all of our questions in this chapter. We only need to go back to Peter's vision on the roof in Jaffa. "*God has shown me that I should not call any man common or unclean*" (Acts 10:28b). He understood the vision as directing him to the (formerly considered unclean) Gentiles. He preached this message without leading them into the Mosaic life style, and they received the Spirit, were filled, spoke in tongues, magnified God, and were immersed in water.

Later, Paul called Peter a hypocrite because at first, he was enjoying table fellowship with Gentiles (Galatians 2:11-12). But when the circumcised believers came, Peter pretended not to be with them. God used him to open the door to Gentiles following Yeshua without full Torah observance, but before his peer Apostles he drew back from what was then a radical position in order to "save face". If Torah for the Gentiles was the mode, the Gentiles would have already been kosher and there would have been no problem between Paul and Peter.

But when I saw that they were not straightforward about the truth of the gospel, I said to Peter before them all "If you, being a Jew, live in the manner of the Gentiles and not as the Jews, why do you compel Gentiles to live as Jews?" Galatians 2:14

What WAS the truth of the gospel? That a Gentile did not have to become a Jew. What is becoming a Jew? Living according to the requirements of Torah. God made it clear in the New Covenant that He is not requiring Gentiles to become Jews in order to follow Yeshua. We must understand Scriptures in their original context. "Becoming a Jew" in the ears of the 1st century Apostles, meant conforming to Torah, including circumcision—the sign of Torah observance. Any convert to Judaism HAD to be circumcised. Controversy began when some Pharisee believers said:

It is necessary to circumcise them and to command them to keep the law of Moses. Acts 15:5

Peter's response, in Acts 15:7-9, was "Hey, these Gentile guys came to faith in Yeshua without converting to Judaism."

[God] *made no distinction between us and them…Now therefore, why do you test God by putting a yoke on the neck of the disciples which neither our fathers nor we were able to bear?* Acts 15:9-10

After a period of pregnant silence, James sums up the situation:

Simon has declared how God…visited the Gentiles to take out of them a people for His name. And with this the words of the prophets agree, just as it is written: "After this I will return and will rebuild the tabernacle of David, which has fallen down; I will rebuild its ruins, and I will set it up; So that the rest of mankind may seek the Lord, even all the Gentiles who are called by my name [quoting Amos 9:11-12]…" Acts 15:14-17

How cool is that? James (whose Hebrew name was *Ya'akov*) understood the entrance of the Gentiles to God's Messianic kingdom as a fulfillment of Amos's ancient prophecy. This gives a resounding witness that the Jewish Apostles were aware of the Lord's intention all along—to include the Gentiles.

Finally, James renders his decision. *"I judge that we should not trouble those from among the Gentiles who are turning to God"* (Acts 15:19). Trouble them about what? The clear context is: <u>trouble them to keep the whole of the law given to Israel</u>. As part of this decision, an authoritative letter is issued. In the letter the new non-Jewish believers are instructed not to eat food from idols, not to engage in any sexual immorality, and not to eat blood or animals that had been strangled. To that he adds, *"Moses is preached and read every Shabbat."* I believe this refers to the moral dimensions of the law. In other words, they did not need to hear about the ten commandments, God's moral law, all over again.

Why was no instruction then given to the Gentiles (in this defining letter) to follow the whole of Torah? There is no such instruction because it was not the design of the Almighty to induct Jesus' Gentile followers into the physical House of Israel. We cannot find one word about a **cov-**

enant responsibility for Gentiles to do so, when it would have been easy to add. In all the epistles to congregations there is not a single direct verse commanding Gentiles to adopt the whole Torah.

Michael Wyschogrod is an Orthodox Jewish professor of philosophy who has specialized in Jewish-Christian relations. The following quote contributes clarity to our discussion.

> "The demands of the Gentile converts in Acts 15:20 have to be understood in light of the rabbinic view of the obligation upon non-Jews. Because of the covenant made at Sinai with Israel, Jews are obligated to obey the commandments of the Torah. Non-Jews, however, are under no such obligation. Instead, they are obligated to obey the so-called Noachide commandments, which the rabbis inferred from Genesis 9."[9]

The decision of the Jerusalem Council is to demand the essence of what later became known as the Noachide commandments (the requirements revealed to Noah for mankind after the flood [Genesis 9:4ff], referenced in the Babylonian Talmud, Sanhedrin 58b-59a). Gentile Yeshua followers were expected to keep these and no more. In so deciding, the Jerusalem church was acting in accordance with the predominant rabbinic thinking of the day.

In their letter to the Gentiles, the Apostles, elders, and brethren emphasize again:

> *..some who went out from us have troubled you with words, unsettling your souls, saying, "You must be circumcised and keep the law"—to whom we gave no such commandment...For it seemed good to the Holy Spirit, and to us, to lay upon you no greater burden than these necessary things.* Acts 15:24, 28

In commenting on this passage, Dr. David Stern writes, "This teaches us that the elements of Torah which apply to Gentiles under the New

Covenant are not the same as those which apply to Jews. It should not surprise us if New Covenant Torah specifies different commandments for Jews and Gentiles. First the Five Books of Moses have commands which apply to some groups and not to others—to the King, but not to his subjects, to *cohanim* (priests) not to other Jews, to men, but not to women."[10]

Mark D. Nanos adds: "The Jerusalem Council...decided that Gentiles were to be admitted as equals into the new community... through faith in Messiah without needing to become Jews...These rules of behavior (Acts 15:19-21; 28-29; 21:24-25)...demonstrated fidelity to the Judaic norms of righteousness that were operative at the time, for Gentiles who had turned from idolatry to the worship of the One God." He continues with amazing clarity. "Gentiles are forbidden to become Jews not because becoming Jewish and keeping Torah are no longer valid acts of faith...they are forbidden because to do so...would implicitly deny his election of Israel and the privilege of Torah..."[11]

It is stated clearly in the biblical text that the Torah is given to Israel. One of the purposes elucidated in the Torah itself is that Israel ought to be a nation set apart from all the other nations. The Torah is not for all, although it does have some commandments that are universal. Not all the Torah is for everyone. What should we do with the very clear text from 1 Corinthians 7:18-20?

> *Was anyone called while circumcised? Let him not become uncircumcised. Was anyone called while uncircumcised? Let him not be circumcised. Circumcision is nothing and uncircumcision is nothing, but keeping the commandments of God is what matters. Let each one remain in the same calling in which he was called.*

As Joseph Shulam, veteran Israeli Bible teacher and Messianic pioneer in Jerusalem, told me: "There is no way to keep respect for the Word of God and at the same time skip over these very clear commands.

In my opinion there are two ways to destroy the Jewish nation. One is assimilation of the Jews to make them Gentiles and make them forget who they really are; and the Church has tried this for 2,000 years. The other way is to get all the Gentiles to pretend to be Jews and to supersede the Jewish nation. If the Gentiles all act like Jews, it will no longer be possible to distinguish who is a Jew or who is not a Jew after one generation. I don't believe that my Bible teaches that this is a good thing. What is more is that I know many dozens of people who have tried it and destroyed their families and their faith in the end."

Later in the Book of Acts, Paul reported to James and the elders what God did among the Gentiles. Since he was "the Apostle" to the Gentiles we can expect him to address this subject during his writings. His answer illustrates the continued life of Jewish practice for Messianic Jews. And it shows that the Gentiles were not required to follow the same way of Moses.

> *...how many myriads of Jews there are who have believed, and they are all zealous for the law; but they have been informed about you that you teach all the Jews who are among the Gentiles to forsake Moses, saying that they ought not to circumcise their children nor to walk according to the customs...But concerning the Gentiles who believe, we have written and decided that they should observe no such thing, except that they should keep themselves from things offered to idols, from blood, from things strangled, and from sexual immorality.* Acts 21:20-21, 25

The Equality of Jews and Gentiles

Paul's perspective concerning the Gentiles was that they were included in God's gracious plan of salvation without having to become Jews. The Apostle affirmed that He is the God of the Jews and the Gentiles (Romans 3:29). In order to make this point, Abraham's faith—while he was still uncircumcised—is the subject of

Romans 4. This was for the expressed purpose of counteracting Jewish pride and the error that Gentiles could not be saved without conversion to Judaism. Then later, in Romans 9-11 Paul deals with the opposite error...to make sure the Gentiles do not exclude the Jews. His conclusion?

There is no distinction between Jew and Greek..."whoever calls on the name of the Lord shall be saved." Romans 10:12-13

In 1 Corinthians 9:19-22 Paul speaks of Gentiles connecting with God apart from Torah. Here he exhorts us to reach out to those without the law as if we ourselves are not under the law, i.e. Gentiles. And by the same token, he applies this truth to the Jewish side. He tells the Corinthians *"...to the Jews I became as a Jew...to those who are under the law, as under the law...to those who are without law* [the Gentiles], *as without law..."* (1 Corinthians 9:20-21). There has been a change with the coming of the New Covenant kingdom whereby the fullness of what is available is offered without the necessity of circumcision for Gentiles (Galatians 5:1-6). This was not the case in the Mosaic order. In this context, Paul gives one declaration which is truly amazing:

And I testify again to every man who becomes circumcised that he is a debtor to keep the whole law. Galatians 5:3

The reverse is also true. There is no such thing as adhering to the law without circumcision. I do not know how it is legitimately possible to escape the weight of this verse and its implications. This was written specifically to Gentile believers, to emphasize that <u>if one is not circumcised he is not obligated to obey the whole law</u>. Paul's statement would make no sense if Gentiles were already obligated to keep the whole law!

The Epistle to the Galatians is written to the Gentiles on this subject. The rabbi, Saul (Paul), is seeking to discourage Gentiles from converting to Judaism (i.e. submitting to Torah and getting circumcised).

Paul is not demanding that all Messianic Jews legalistically observe every detail of the law. Elsewhere (1 Corinthians 7:19 and Philippians 3:3-9 among many passages) he states that law-keeping does not save us. He is seeking to dissuade Gentile circumcision and the responsibility of keeping all the Torah.

In Colossians, Paul discusses the ordinances of food, drink and festivals. He writes *"So let no one judge you in food or in drink or regarding a festival or a new moon or Sabbaths"* (Colossians 2:16). What is the clear meaning of these verses? It is that we are forbidden to judge a believer based on what holidays he observes or doesn't observe. The issue is Messiah. Of course, this does not mean that it's unavailable to the Gentile disciple. But it says to me that we are not to judge, criticize, demean, or think less of them.

The advent of the New Covenant changes the dynamic in applying Torah statements about Gentiles. The inclusion of Gentiles into the house of faith, without circumcision and without conversion to Judaism, embraces them without the requirement of Mosaic observance. This is the clear sense of Acts 15, 21, and Paul's epistles.

Neither Male nor Female...The Continuing Distinction

For you are all sons of God through faith in Messiah Yeshua...There is neither Jew nor Greek, there is neither slave nor free, there is neither male nor female... Galatians 3:26,28

Logically and practically, we would all admit that male and female still exist in different forms. In spite of what we might understand from a superficial reading of the text, the point here is that there is no preference in spiritual value between men and women, between employers and employees, nor between Jews and non-Jews. God does not want His Jewish children to wish they were Gentiles. Likewise, He does not want His Gentile children jealous of His Jewish children. We are equally beloved in His eyes. The extraordinary friendship to which we are called, now, at the end of the age, demands that we treasure each other as we are.

Saul's statement to the Galatians is helpful. For those who belong to Messiah, these distinctions neither interfere with fellowship nor do they create higher/lower categories of people. The parallelism demands equal application. There are still Jews and Gentiles. What then is the difference? The Jew is related to God not only through faith in Yeshua, but also through the historic covenants made by God with our ancestors. These covenants were made specifically to call us out as a people, to bring Messiah forth and to establish the nation of Israel. To require Gentiles to be Jews is the same as requiring women to be men. There is one clear exception: a Messianic Jew and a believing Gentile who marry become one flesh. We see this in Romans 10:12-13 and in Colossians 3:10-11.

There is not a single word in the New Testament that exhorts Gentiles to circumcision, feasts, purity laws, Sabbaths, fast days and more. At the same time it is clear in the New Testament that these practices were, and continue to be, the way of life given to all Jews, including Messianic Jews.

In all of this discussion, we want to keep in mind the Acts 10 Caesarea breakthrough, Peter's experience in the house of Cornelius. When they embraced Israel's Messiah, it fulfilled vital *Tanakh* passages that God's light would shine upon the Gentiles (see Chapter 2). From that point on, Gentiles are invited to enter Yeshua's everlasting kingdom, and share as equal partners with His Jewish followers. The spiritual equality of Jew and Gentile in the Messiah is a monumental change. It rocked the Messianic community in the first century (see Acts 11-15) and ultimately brought salvation to the entire world.

Yet the New Covenant does not present a homogenization of Jew and Gentile for the purpose of equality. There remains a unique calling and identity for the Jewish people. This fulfills God's covenant promises. The attempt to bring Gentiles fully into a "Torah lifestyle" violates the order God has set forth.

We cannot stand for both a Zionist formulation that calls for Jewish return to the land, and God's covenant promise to literal Israel, while at the same time expecting that all Gentile believers need to adhere to Torah.

What about Gentiles in a Messianic Jewish Congregation?

On the one hand, God's heart is to bring Jews and Gentiles together as one "bride." On the other hand, we have presented the principle of an ongoing distinction between Jewish and Gentile disciples of Yeshua. The majority of Messianic Jewish congregations include generous percentages of non-Jewish believers. What is to be the approach of those non-Jewish members? How can a Gentile participate in the biblical Jewish celebrations of a life cycle based on Torah and identifying with literal Israel?

Ruth helps us to understand the calling of these valued members of the Messianic community. She never claimed to be Jewish by birth, or a member of "spiritual Israel." But, by marrying into the nation of Israel, she adopted the way of life maintained by her husband, Boaz. In so doing, she affirmed her earlier declaration (Ruth 1:16-17), that she had made Naomi's people "her people." Ruth's commitment was to the God of Israel and to the people of Israel. By marrying Boaz, she took on the customs and the practices of her husband's land. Her heart was covenanted with the People of the Book.

Similarly, the non-Jewish members of Messianic Jewish congregations are declaring their identification with the calling of Jewish believers, to return Yeshua to His original framework as the Son of David, the Son of Abraham. As long as he does not claim to be saved by "works of the law," the Gentile living and worshiping regularly among Messianic Jews is free to celebrate a Torah-based lifestyle with the Jewish members of his spiritual community. Otherwise, the congregation would be divided within itself. Yet, a healthy, non-prejudicial attitude of heart is essential within every New Covenant fellowship. Elsewhere, I have emphasized the necessity of being secure with each other and loving each other as we are. All the more, this applies to a Messianic Jewish congregation, which is seeking to recover the blessing of the original Israel-centered *kehila* (congregation, community).

Messianic Jewish congregations around the world experience a high level of interest, participation and membership from non-Jewish believers, whether it be in occasional fellowship, involvement for a season, or in long-term commitment. The goal is that in every case it is for healthy reasons, and that they not become embroiled in confusion, superiority or inferiority. It is interesting to note that non-Jewish participation in some level of Jewish religious life was a known phenomenon even 2,000 years ago, as evidenced by Paul's interactions with Jews and "devout Greeks" in the synagogue of Thessalonica in Acts 17:1-4. (See also John 12:20 and Acts 14:1.)

If the Torah is Mandatory for Gentiles, It Creates an Anti-Church Attitude of Judgment

Gentiles for Torah argue that all believers should keep the whole law, because such a life is superior to that based only on the New Covenant. When the same folks view their observance of Torah as superior to that of other Gentiles who do not, their position easily leads to cynicism regarding the traditions of Christian followers of Yeshua. The blanket denigration of the Church as pagan is inaccurate, wrong and unhelpful to God's restoration of Israel. The disunity caused by claiming that the Church is pagan is alarming and damaging. It is this author's view that proponents of "Torah for Gentiles," though they may personally be humble, are promoting an arrogant and divisive doctrine.

This pendulum swing, seeking to convince all church members that their customs are wrong and abhorrent to God, does injury to the unity of the Body and to the prophetic restoration of a Jewish-rooted New Testament. Many church leaders have shared with me their wariness of Christians who have suddenly become champions of Torah for the Gentiles. They and their flocks have been wounded by believers criticizing their teaching, their authority, and their relevance. Is there need for a more positive understanding of the Hebraic roots of New Testament faith? Certainly. Can humble servants of the Lord contribute the integration of biblical feasts and the inseparable nature of *Tanakh* and New Covenant, to their churches? Definitely. In our enthusiasm, however, we must be respectful and teachable. Ultimately, "who" we are and the "flavor" of our communication can speak so loudly that "what" we are saying cannot be heard.

Although I believe that many aspects of Torah are universal, there are also many aspects of Torah distinct to the Jewish people. This basic distinction between Jew and Gentile is maintained in the New Covenant. Jews are called to covenant responsibilities that relate to the whole Torah. Gentiles in Yeshua are not called in the same way, but certainly to the responsibility of universal Torah as typified in the teaching of Yeshua and the epistles of the New Covenant Scriptures.

Chapter Eleven

Israel's Unknown Hero and the Egyptians

Who Set the Table for Joseph's Brothers?

And Joseph said to his brothers, "Please come near to me." So they came near. Then he said "I am Joseph, your brother, whom you sold into Egypt. But now, do not therefore be grieved or angry with yourselves because you sold me here; for God sent me before you to preserve life." Genesis 45:4-5

One night I flew into the Kansas City Airport. Inside, I saw a group of people with signs: "Welcome home R.C....We love you, Ray... You're our hero." I was curious. They were lined up, smiling. Then I understood.

There was a young man in the defining desert camouflage US soldier's uniform—hugging a young woman with a baby while others cheered and waved. It was one of America's servicemen, home from dangerous missions in Iraq.

What if no one had been there? What if that soldier had risked his life, even been wounded, seen death and done it all for his country and family—yet not a soul bothered to meet him at the airport. Poignant? Bring a tear to the eye?

Yeshua has not been "met at the airport" for nearly 2,000 years. The God of Israel is weeping. Can we enter His broken heart? Is it not Jacob's heart, broken for his lost, "dead" son Joseph? How did Jacob feel when they said "He's alive!"? I would like to put this analogy in very practical terms. How does it look to an educated Israeli today, some thirty-seven centuries after Joseph was rejected by his brothers?

Israeli Governement Official Hears About Joseph and Jesus

A key official in the government of a northern Israeli city once asked me a startling question. "What is it that you believe, as a Messianic Jew? What is the basis of your faith?" I thought for a moment. Then I told him the story of Joseph. Growing up in a very observant home, of course he knew this story—perhaps better than I did. When I drew the parallel between Joseph being unrecognizable to his brothers and Yeshua being unrecognizable to His Jewish brothers today, my friend was speechless. He had no disagreement, but neither was he ready for my application of the story. The similarity of Joseph's experience with his brothers, to the unknown identity of Yeshua as our true Messiah was planted way back then. It is the brilliance of the God of Israel, who knows the end from the beginning and places types and shadows of the future so that we can catch them later.

The sequence foreshadowed in the Joseph story must take place for Yeshua to truly be the Messiah. If we don't "reject" Him at first, He is not the real one. Ironic, isn't it? He is the unknown hero.

Sometimes Christians ask "But why did the Jews not know who Jesus was and accept Him?" First, it's always easier to see in hindsight. What is obvious to us after we know or believe something was not so clear before. Second, the question ignores the fact that Yeshua did not come as a flashy figure. Isaiah even says *"And when we see Him, there is no beauty that we should desire Him"* (Isaiah 53:2b). Third, as I'm seeking to point out, if Jesus was received by the majority as Messiah, it would have short-circuited the entire plan of God.

Please consider the following passages. They highlight this expectation unmistakably. (Emphasis added)

The stone which the builders rejected has become the chief cornerstone. This was the Lord's doing; It is marvelous in our eyes. This is the day the Lord has made; We will rejoice and be glad in it. Psalm 118:22-24

He is despised and rejected by men…we did not esteem Him…we esteemed Him stricken, smitten by God, and afflicted. Isaiah 53:3-4b

… they will look on Me whom they pierced. Yes, they will mourn for Him as one mourns for his only son… Zechariah 12:10

Later, in the New Covenant, Paul the Apostle devotes the 11th chapter of his letter to the believers in Rome (especially vv.11-15; 25-26), to this sometimes overlooked "promise." But as Solomon declared in dedicating the Temple *"There has not failed one word of all His good promise…"* (1 Kings 8:56). The fact is that this national "failure" to embrace the Messiah was not only seen from afar, but figures directly into the Christian relationship with Israel. In the same verses in which Paul says that our eyes will be blinded, he talks about the Gentiles provoking us to jealousy—i.e. they will be wearing the garments of salvation that were always intended for us!

Bottom line, what are the key points of Joseph's life that create a picture like that of Yeshua? Here's my list. It's only one out of many. I draw out this parallel because it is so vivid, and so relevant to finding the role of the Gentiles in Israel's salvation.

JOSEPH as a type of JESUS:

1. Chosen by his father and uniquely loved
2. Given early revelation of a special mission to save his people
3. Misunderstood and rejected by his brothers (a la Isaiah 53)
4. Thrown into a pit/grave as dead
5. Raised from that pit in the likeness of resurrection
6. Taken to the Gentiles
7. After some years lifted to a position of highest authority among the Gentiles (at age 30), becoming the "Savior of the world" Genesis 41:53-57!
8. Appearance "changes" to look like an Egyptian/Gentile
9. Brothers, the sons of Jacob, come at a time of famine (Amos 8:11)
10. They do not recognize their brother, and return to their father. Jacob typifies the Jewish response to a painful history *"Joseph is no more, Simeon is no more, and you want to take Benjamin. All these things are against me"* (Genesis 42:36). He sounds like Naomi! The WHOLE WORLD knew Joseph as the source of bread. But his heart ached for his "Jewish" brothers. **The story will not be complete until his family is reunited.**
11. When they finally return, they are bringing Benjamin (then favored at Joseph's table). Joseph is clearly "wooing them back" with each step in the encounter. *"Joseph saw his brothers and recognized them, but he acted as a stranger to them"* (Genesis 42:7).
12. Joseph weeps over his brothers repeatedly (Genesis 43:30, seeing Benjamin, and Genesis 45:1-8 finally revealing himself to his brothers). *"God sent me before you to preserve a posterity for you in the earth and to save your lives by a great deliverance. So now it was not you who sent me here, but God..."* (Genesis 45:7-8a). Wow! This verse is super prophetic when you apply it to the Greater Joseph, Yeshua.

It is exactly here, at the recognition of Joseph as the rejected brother, now embraced by the world as its "savior" that the Egyptians' role is highlighted. We do well to imagine the scene. Joseph, having begun as a slave, has risen to the office of prime minister. He is responsible for distributing food during a time of world-wide famine (Genesis 41:54-57). Jacob, seeing this and knowing that the camp will soon die of starvation, sends the remaining sons to buy grain in Egypt. When they arrive, Joseph recognizes his brothers but they do not recognize him.

A series of incidents ensues in which Joseph accomplishes several things. One, he brings his brothers to the humble realization of their guilt in long ago rejecting him. Two, he prepares the way emotionally for them to discover who he really is (after several nerve-wracking situations in which they risk execution). Three, he sets before them a banquet. And in Joseph's so doing, we can see the importance of the role to which the Egyptians are raised.

We must remember that in the ancient world, the place occupied by those who served the top leaders was an honored one. One was not allowed to serve food and drink to the king, or high government officials without top security clearance and much favor. In the intrigue and brutality of those courts, the servants had to be trustworthy and were, at times, the confidantes of those being served. We are reminded of Nehemiah's place as the one serving wine to King Artaxerxes (Nehemiah 2:1-2). Abraham's personal servant, Eliezer, was even entrusted with the task of finding a wife for his master's son (Genesis 24:2-4)!

Now, we return to Joseph's banquet for his brothers. The first banquet takes place in Genesis 43, after the sons of Jacob return to Egypt for food at the insistence of their father. Very reluctantly, the old man releases Benjamin, per Joseph's clever request. Seeing Benjamin, Joseph orders a feast (Genesis 43:16). It is significant that the banquet takes place in Joseph's house. If we are to see this as a scenario that previews Yeshua revealing Himself to His brothers, we must see that Yeshua is the "host." The setting for self-revelation is of His making. Joseph/ Yeshua is creating the experience for just the right time, with maximum impact. Before sending them off again, Joseph has his own silver cup placed in Benjamin's sack, reducing the brothers to stark terror and mourning when they discover the cup (Genesis 44:13). They are next seen in Joseph's presence, falling before him on the ground. This act is a prophetic foreshadowing of the worship Israel's sons will ultimately give to Yeshua.

Chapter 45 begins with Joseph not being able to restrain himself any longer. Imagine this as our Lord, the Messiah—separated for so many long centuries from His own nation. What a picture this gives us of the heart of Yeshua! Joseph shows us the agony of this separation. Weeping aloud, Joseph says *"I am Joseph; does my father still live?"* The brothers are blown away. They are dumbstruck. One moment they are being confronted for lying and the next moment they are confronted with the complete shock of Egypt's leader unmasking himself as—could this really be?—their brother, Joseph!

I love it when Joseph says *"Please come near to me"* (Genesis 45:4). They do; and he tells them not to be upset that they originally sold him into slavery. Transferring this prophetic picture, Yeshua is going to speak to His people, revealing Himself as the Messiah. As we recognize Him, He will draw us near to Him in weeping fellowship. What an incredible day that will be.

But what about the servants? They could hear the agonized weeping of Joseph. They knew something out of the ordinary was happening. What was their role? They had earlier laid an entire feast before these sons of Jacob. Now, after hearing about the dramatic reunion, there was rejoicing.

...it was heard in Pharaoh's house, saying, "Joseph's brothers have come." So it pleased Pharaoh and his servants well. Genesis 45:16

Furthermore, Pharaoh commanded that carts be taken to Jacob's territory to bring him back to Egypt. The Egyptians provided the carts to bless Jacob after Joseph's identity was revealed. What a picture of the Gentile role in Israel's salvation! Through Pharaoh and his workforce, Joseph's brothers were served. We could say that these Gentiles were used by God to set the stage for the revelation, the reunion, and the subsequent celebration on the part of Jacob and his sons. That is no small part to fulfill in the completion of God's ancient plan.

Solomon's passionate prayer as he dedicates the Temple reminds me of Joseph's tearful reaction to seeing his brothers after many years. In his youth, Joseph was given prophetic expectation of being raised to an unusual position in his family. To his amazement this took place once his brothers realized who he was. Solomon also received a promise, albeit from his father, that he would build a house for God. Finally, that house, the Temple, is finished. Solomon gives thanks to the Living God:

> *Blessed be the Lord, who has given rest to His people Israel, according to* <u>*all that He promised*</u>*. There has not failed one word of all His good promise, which He promised through His servant Moses.* 1 Kings 8:56

Acknowledging that the Lord keeps His promises, Israel's king anticipates the statement of Isaiah, generations later.

> *So shall my word be that goes forth from my mouth; it shall not return to me void, but it shall accomplish what I please and it shall prosper in the thing for which I sent it.* Isaiah 55:11

God has planted promises in His word. It is now time to see them come to fruition. The most important of all God's promises is that He will send His Messiah to Israel and the nations. This Messiah will bear the sins of the entire world and yet have power over death (Isaiah 53).

The promise of Israel's ultimate recognition of her Messiah (Zechariah 12:10) cannot be fulfilled without the essential role played by Yeshua's international disciples. They, like Joseph's servants of old, are to be aware of the special visitors He is about to receive in His house.

Chapter Twelve

The Cup of Covenant Friendship

The True, Eternal Basis of Our Partnership

So David went on and became great, and the Lord God of hosts was with him. Then Hiram, king of Tyre, sent messengers to David and cedar trees, and carpenters and masons. And they built David a house. 2 Samuel 5:10-11

...at the end of twenty years...Solomon had built the two houses, the house of the Lord and the king's house (Hiram the king of Tyre had supplied Solomon with cedar and cypress and gold, as much as he desired), that King Solomon then gave Hiram twenty cities in the land of the Galilee. 1 Kings 9:10-11

I held the goblet of wine aloft in my hand. Feeling a tenderness of heart, as I always do during the Messiah's Supper, I surprised myself. Sitting on the front row, to the side of our sanctuary, was a German pastor with whom I'd become good friends. Spontaneously, not stopping to analyze what was happening, I invited him to come and stand next to me, in front of the entire congregation. I have never done anything similar before or since. But when Hans (German-born, Pastor Hans

Scholz) responded by joining me and holding the same cup aloft with me, his hand under mine, something happened. Heaven came near. Unknowingly, we had touched the heart of God.

A German disciple of Yeshua, not just a non-Jew, but a member of the society that had only a few decades earlier been responsible for the death of 6,000,000 Jews, stood with me on Israeli soil in a dramatic moment of God-authored unity. The Cup of the Lord provides a degree of atonement and of deep reconciliation that no other earthly substance or symbol does. The blood of Messiah cleanses us and removes every barrier between us and God, but also between us and each other. I cannot describe how close I felt to Hans in that moment. It was a gift of realization. I realized that we were ONE.

This was much more than joining Hans and me in outward reconciliation—a mere cessation of hostilities. Rather, it was the fullness of reconciliation. We had become "blood brothers" sharing a common identity as sons of one Father. While the history of our nations impacts reality in painful and still incomprehensible ways, God is able to redeem. In that moment there was a redemption, a brotherhood, a commonality of purpose in submitting to the God of Israel and His Messiah. Nothing else, and no one else, can achieve that.

The Last Supper and the Intersection of the Covenants

As a very young believer I was reading the account of the Last Supper one day. Suddenly I snapped to the fact that this "supper" was none other than the Passover *Seder* meal. I was "blown away." Looking up from the Bible, it seemed that the axis of the earth had shifted. Was this possible? Was Yeshua's last meal with His disciples in fact the Passover meal commanded by the God of Israel in Exodus 12 and eaten by the families of Israel for the last 3,400 years? It was no other. If it is so, I reasoned, then there are a number of fundamental, influential truths that must be reckoned with.

1. The "Old" and "New" Testaments are inseparably linked. What a wonderful concept that was!
2. Yeshua was declaring Himself to be Jewish and embracing our history as His own.
3. This absolutely pivotal event, the crucifixion, was forever being interwoven with the record of God's saving acts toward His people, Israel.
4. He chose the Passover *matzoh* and the wine as the elements of our deep fellowship. Physically partaking of them declares our newfound bond with each other, based on His loving sacrifice for us all.

How are Jew and Gentile to really come together, in full trust, to bring about Israel's redemption? Given the history of our relationship since the end of the first century, this question does not yield an easy answer. The historic relationship between the Church, "established in Jesus' name," and the Jewish people, has been a uniquely rancorous and lethal chronicle. What excruciating irony that the Jews, the natural family of Israel's Messiah, Jesus, have been persecuted by Gentiles carrying His banner! The previous paragraphs hold, in utterly refreshing contrast, what I believe to be the key to a God-initiated, long-awaited reconciliation/restoration. When we know each other as blood brothers and our relationship is a friendship based on the eternal blood of the Lamb, then He brings us together. It is His idea, neither yours nor mine. *"With men this is impossible, but with God all things are possible"* (Matthew 19:26).

What I learned from holding the cup with Hans was that Yeshua's sacrifice is the lasting and most effective tool in bringing us together in the purposes of God. The death and resurrection of Yeshua form the cords of covenant that tie our hearts together as recipients of the same grace. We have unique, yet fully complimentary, callings. It must be this way. In order to fulfill those callings, we need to celebrate and comprehend communion as the starting point for our friendship. We need to be secure with each other, to be freed from jealousy (see Chapter 9: The Return of the Lost Son).

We have arrived at the final chapter of this book. Here is my conclusion. The only way for the nations to fulfill their divinely commanded role in Israel's redemption is by coming into a full covenant friendship with their Jewish brothers and sisters in Messiah. What do I mean by covenant friendship? Many have written on the subject, but none, in my opinion, more clearly or compellingly than my buddy, Asher Intrater. He makes the following statements that help us understand the term "covenant friendship."

"God's principle of relationship is covenant."[12]

"There is something about the nature of a blood covenant that leaves a deeper impression on the psyche than almost anything else."[13]

"The model of Yeshua having given His life (in blood sacrifice) looms large behind all of our individual interactions with one another."[14]

If we are to see "all Israel saved" and the Messiah Himself return, there will have to be much more than a superficial "peace-making" between the Jewish and the Gentile communities of Yeshua. The power of heaven is released when we live selflessly and when we acknowledge the full nature of God dwelling within every member of His kingdom. Is it possible to do that and at the same time acknowledge the pivotal role to which the God of Israel has called His people, Israel?

Yes, it must be possible, though we may have to fight for it. Like the friendship of David and Jonathan, our friendship comes at a weighty price. A Jew must humble himself to accept that without the non-Jews the ultimate plan of God is incomplete. A Gentile must also humble himself to agree that the plan of God is not complete without the return of the Jewish people, both to the land and to the King that God has provided.

True friendship is placing the same value on the life of one's friend as on one's own life. David and Jonathan pledged themselves to each other in this way. They were ready to lay down their lives for each other.

Greater love has no one than this, than to lay down one's life for his friends. John 15:13

How far am I willing to go? Do I only love Gentiles because I think they are part of God's inescapable plan and that our cooperation will get me where I need to go? Or do the Gentile Christians only tolerate their Jewish brothers in Messiah because He will not return without their "joining the club?"

To answer these and other knotty questions, we must return to the scene of Jesus and the disciples on the night before He was pierced. They were not in a banquet hall. They were sitting on pillows, on the floor, in intimate and unhurried pleasure. Food and drink were plentiful. The light was low. They were being bound together as never before by their Master, who purposefully seized on the depth of the occasion to heighten an already ancient, national meal. Yeshua was drawing them together into the New Covenant in His blood. He took them beyond their previous concepts of dedication to the God of Israel and to one another. He did it by offering His own life. And He did it in the setting of a covenant meal that affirmed their need for Him and for each other.

Table Fellowship is Sacred

Once, during a dinner break from a conference on Israel and the Church, I sat across from a brother whose walk with the Lord and practical wisdom always stimulates me. His name is Phil. He happens to be a Gentile disciple of Jesus, but that was not in either of our minds while we thoroughly enjoyed our meal together. As we ate and talked, our hearts were woven together in a delicious, delightful way. At some point we recognized what an amazing time we were having, over the seemingly commonplace activity of consuming food and beverage. It struck us both that we were experiencing the rich pleasure of the Lord in our shared covenant. We inadvertently discovered an extraordinary passageway between heaven and earth. The memory of that experience still causes us to smile, when we realize that God was treating us to a meal of covenant celebration.

The leisurely dinner Phil and I shared provides a preview for us all. Let me explain. We began with the question "What about us?" That question implies the chance of someone being left out. No one will be left out! When the King comes to earth, we will sit together at one table—covenant brothers and sisters from all the nations together with His Jewish disciples—laughing, enjoying, and spreading His salvation forever.

The priority of international Christian involvement in God's end-time scenario in Israel is the subject of this book. We conclude where we began, with the friendship of two men, a Gentile (King Hiram) and a Jew (King Solomon, preceded by his father, David). We Jews and Gentiles are called first, and foundationally, to a covenant of friendship. Without this, all the strategy, theology, and politics in the world will not achieve the turning of Israel's heart to Yeshua.

Through the kind of friendship/communion/cooperation enjoyed by Hiram and Solomon, we will see, in the immediate years to come, the ultimate fulfillment of our kingdom callings. Then, the glory of God will come back to Israel in the person of Yeshua and He will be King of all the earth. It is to this glory He is drawing us. He is drawing us together—inexorably—to achieve the fullness of His all-inclusive plan.

Endnotes

[1] *Yeshua*, the Hebrew of Jesus, is the primary way I've referred to the Lord throughout this book. When, however, I'm speaking of His role in the historic Church or among Gentile believers, I have used Jesus for reasons of emphasis and context.

[2] H. J. Katzenstein, *The History of Tyre*, The Schocken Institute for Jewish Research, Jerusalem, 1973 [quoted in www.glbet-el.org/.../ Hiram%20king%20Of%20Tyr%20site.pdf].

[3] Gruber, *The Separation of Church & Faith, Volume One: Copernicus and the Jews*. p. 242.

[4] See Gruber's brilliant analysis of the deterioration of the initial Jew-Gentile partnership in *The Church and the Jews*, Elijah Publishing, Hanover, NH, 1997. (From the introduction, p.vii ff).

[5] *Replacement Theology* is the notion that the Church "replaces" Israel because of her unfaithfulness. In this formula, the Christian Church takes the blessings promised to Israel and leaves her the curses.

[6] Introduction, Silberling, *"The Ephraimite Error,"* (http://www.seedofabraham.org/downloads/ephraimite error.pdf).

[7] Juster & Resnik, *"One Law Movements,"* p. 2.

[8] W.D. Davies, *Paul and Rabbinic Judaism*, p.67.

[9] M. Wyschogrod, in *Evangelicals and Jews in Conversation on Scripture, Theology and History*, edited by Tanenbaum, Wilson and Rudin, p.44.

[10] Dr. David Stern, *Messianic Jewish Manifesto*, p.156.

[11] Mark D. Nanos, *The Mystery of Romans*, p.167 & p.184.

[12] Asher Intrater, *Covenant Relationships*, p.32

[13] Ibid, p.27

[14] Ibid, p.32

Bibliography

Davies, W.D., Paul and *Rabbinic Judaism*, Fortress Press, Philadelphia, 1980.

Gruber, Daniel, *The Church and the Jews*, Elijah Publishing, Hanover, NH, 1997.

Gruber, Daniel, *The Separation of Church & Faith, Volume One: Copernicus and the Jews*, Elijah Publishing, Hanover, NH, 2005.

Intrater, Asher, *Covenant Relationships*, 1989, Destiny Image, Shippensburg, PA.

Juster, Dr. Daniel and Resnik, Russell, *"One Law Movements,"* (http://www.umjc.org/ home-mainmenu-1/faqs-mainmenu-58/14-umjc-faq/24-is-the-torah-only-for-jews).

Katzenstein, H.J., *The History of Tyre*, The Schocken Institute for Jewish Research, Jerusalem, 1973.

Nanos, Mark D., *The Mystery of Romans*, Fortress Press, Minneapolis, 1996.

Silberling, Dr. Kay, *"The Ephraimite Error"* (http://www.seedofabraham.org/downloads/ephraimite error.pdf).

Stern, Dr. David, *Messianic Jewish Manifesto*, Jewish New Testament Publications, Jerusalem, 1988.

Wyschogrod, Michael, in Chapter 2 of *Evangelicals and Jews in Conversation*, Edited by Tannenbaum, Wilson, and Rudin, Baker House, Grand Rapids, 1978.

Acknowledgments

It is a luxury to write a book. I could not have done it without a huge amount of assistance. Therefore, it is with a tender heart that I acknowledge all those who helped and encouraged me, whether I mention their name or not.

My first acknowledgment is one of everlasting gratitude to my wife and life partner, Connie Kind Shishkoff. When someone agrees to spend a lifetime with you it is a marathon journey. We've traveled forty-four years together already! Not only that, but she's an amazing artist. (Connie's illustrations adorn the beginning of each chapter.) Thanks, dearest.

Our son, David, in addition to being one of this book's editors, has coached me tirelessly in the design and completion of *What About Us?* I really enjoy working with you! To all of our children and their spouses (David and Orit, Hannah and Avishalom, Avi and Sigal), as well as our nine treasured grandchildren, my heart is full of love and appreciation for all the encouragement and affection you give me.

I've been blessed with a phenomenal administrative assistant, Leora. She deserves abundant recognition. She not only served as one of the editors, but she helps keep me organized from week to week—and has done so for many years. Todah rabbah!

To the other editors, Dr. Larry Brunner, Pamela Bernstein, Marty Shoub, and Michael Weiner, I say "Bravo!" Your dedication to review the manuscript word for word has made this a far better work than it was at the beginning. Acclaim also goes to those who gave their endorsement and those who interceded for this maiden effort in publishing a book. That reminds me, I'm grateful to Tim Taylor of Burkhart Books, who shepherded the volume through the critical final stage, causing it to roll off the presses.

And, of course, I want to acknowledge the long-standing support of our congregation, Tents of Mercy, its elders, and the daughter congregations and their spiritual leaders that have sprung up from it. Last, but not least, I am grateful to all our friends in the nations. Their friendship and enthusiastic embrace of us as their Messianic Jewish brothers in Israel, has inspired me to write this book. It is my hope that many more will catch the wave that these men and women of faith have already been riding.

These remarks would be incomplete without giving glory and thanksgiving to our King, Yeshua, who brought me from the dark night of my soul, to His light.

About the Author

Eitan and Connie Shishkoff came to faith in Yeshua in 1972 while living the hippie lifestyle in the mountains of New Mexico, USA. From 1981-1992 Eitan served at Beth Messiah Messianic Congregation in Maryland. During the dramatic ex-odus of Jews from the former Soviet Union, Eitan received a vision from the Lord. He was shown a desert oasis, representing a ministry of mercy to the multitudes of immigrants about to arrive in Israel.

In 1992, the Shishkoff family moved to Israel. Three years later, the dream of serving the needy immigrant and native Israeli community became a reality. They moved to the Haifa Bay area and began Tents of Mercy Congregation (*Ohalei Rachamim*). Drawn to the first century model of congregation-planting, the Tents of Mercy leadership team has fostered the equipping and release of new leaders who have established four additional congregations, creating a network of covenanted ministries.

Eitan and Connie have four children and nine grandchildren, who all live in Israel.

Tents of Mercy

I will restore the tents of Jacob and have mercy on his dwelling places.
Jeremiah 30:18

Our vision is to be an oasis for Israel's returning exiles and for her native-born sons and daughters. In the ancient Near East the oasis was an absolutely vital center of refuge, supply, healing, equipping and sending out. This vision is being fulfilled as:

A Humanitarian Aid Center, providing practical assistance to new immigrants, operating out of an industrial warehouse. We supply relief through the distribution of food, clothing, household items, toys and baby supplies.

A Sharing Community Meeting in House Groups (Acts 2:42-47), which seek the healing and equipping of each member for the work of the Lord. Ours is a community of varied origins, illustrating the Book of Ruth paradigm: Israel's end-time harvest comes when Jew and Gentile unite in Messiah.

A Messianic Synagogue Celebrating the Torah Roots of our New Covenant faith, (Jeremiah 31:31-33) embracing Jesus as Israel's Messiah, declaring, "Yeshua, Come Home!"

A Tabernacle of Priestly Worship and Intercession where God's presence is sought passionately, because God said *He would meet with us at the tabernacle* (Exodus 29:42-43). As priests we must cry out *"Spare your people, O Lord"* (Joel 2:17)!

A Congregation-Planting Center, in the apostolic pattern of extending God's kingdom through sending out teams to do humanitarian aid, evangelism and congregation-planting in unreached areas of Israel.

Tents of Mercy is seeking Israel's salvation through planting indigenous, Hebrew-speaking congregations in Yeshua's homeland. We have a special focus on the Galilee and currently have five congregations functioning in that area.

The Spirit of God is restoring apostolic life to Israel. The apostolic blueprint recorded in the Book of Acts is our template for establishing new congregations. In His mercy, God promised to bring back Israel's exiles. Our calling is to be an oasis of provision amidst the hardships that challenge Israel's new citizens.

Is it not to share your bread with the hungry, and that you bring to your house the poor who are cast out; when you see the naked that you cover him? Isaiah 58:7

Our humanitarian services include:
- Humanitarian Aid Warehouse and Distribution Centers
- Pro-Life Counseling Offices
- Soup Kitchens for the Poor
- Assistance to Holocaust Survivors

Tents of Mercy is a partnership of Israel and the Nations. Israel's prophets saw the active partnership of the nations in her future physical and spiritual restoration. This partnership is vital towards hastening the return of Yeshua. We are seeing this wonderfully fulfilled in the Tents of Mercy! Friends from every continent are participating with us in the miracle of Israel's rebirth.

For more information see: www.tentsofmercy.org. Our work is in full covenant cooperation with Tikkun Ministries International, Revive Israel and Gateways Beyond.